Emotional Disorders:

An Outline Guide to Diagnosis and Pharmacological Treatment

Third Edition

WITHDRAWN

by Alberto DiMascio, Ph.D. and Harold L. Goldberg, M.D.

Medical Economics Company **MEBI** **Book Division** Oradell, N.J. 07649

Library of Congress Cataloging in Publication Data

DiMascio, Alberto, date
   Emotional disorders

   Includes bibliographical references.
   1. Psychopharmacology. 2. Mental illness—Diagnosis. I. Goldberg, Harold L., joint author. II. Ti-
tle. [DNLM: 1. Mental disorders—Diagnosis.
2. Mental disorders—Drug therapy. 3. Psychopharmacology. WM402 D582e]
RC483.D55 1980   616.89   80-20629
ISBN 0-87489-255-4

ISBN 0-87489-255-4

Medical Economics Company
Oradell, New Jersey 07649

First Edition   October 1976
Second Edition   August 1977
Third Edition   January 1981

Printed in the United States of America

Contents

Foreword

There is a widespread feeling that we are in the midst of a third revolution in mental health care. The "first revolution" is usually considered to be the freeing of madmen and madwomen from their chains, following the French Revolution. The "second revolution" is most often related to the Freudian enlightenment of more recent times. In the first revolution, release of the mentally ill from physical bondage was the essence; in the second, their release from mental bondage.

Of what does the third great revolution consist? There are so many currents of change around us, it is difficult to make sense out of the confusion. Is the third revolution a function of the "Great Awakening" of government and the public to the welfare of oppressed, disenfranchised, minority peoples and the recognition that the mentally ill, the retarded, the alcoholic, and the drug dependent are parts of this minority?

Is the third revolution, therefore, a sociopolitical one wherein the "Great Awakening" or "Great Acceptance" is being translated into deinstitutionalization, dehospitalization, community-based treatment, and a growing concern for social, familial, and ecological factors in mental disease? The remarkable phasedown of hospital populations, the phasing out of some mental institutions, and the great expansion of ambulatory care—together with outreach efforts into homes, schools, and industries—certainly support that notion.

There are those, however, who feel that the third revolution is more properly related to the recent impressive therapeutic breakthroughs in the somatic and pharmacological spheres. Without the fortunate discoveries in these fields, it is claimed, psychiatry would still have relatively little therapeutic potency, however much it may have increased understanding of the patient's psychodynamics through the Freudian enlightenment. The acute and powerful effects of the new drugs have really impressed the public, raised hopes about the future of mental illness, and encouraged government to be more generous with its resources. Without the antipsychotics, the antidepressants, and the anxiolytics, the sharp depopulation of our mental hospitals would not have occurred, and it would be impossible to keep so many discharged patients in the community.

Proponents of the pharmacological revolution argue that most of the significant sociopolitical changes are really based on therapeutic discoveries in the laboratories and clinics of psychopharmacology. Without pharmacological tools to control deviant and socially repulsive behavior, society would force the mentally ill back into hospitals, and the old wall of resistance and prejudice against them would rise again.

Effectiveness of the antidepressants has opened new vistas of pharmacological application. It is now claimed that literally millions of Americans who are subject to mood swings that impair their lives may eventually benefit from the antidepressants, particularly lithium.

There have been other major consequences of the psychopharmacological revolution. One is the enormous stimulation of research in the biological domain and the consequent fruitful collaboration of scientists from diverse basic disciplines with clinicians. Many promising leads have been uncovered and are now hotly pursued in the fields of biochemistry, pharmacology, ethology, neurophysiology, and clinical psychiatry. There is much to kindle the hope for a more rational and scientific therapeusis in the near future.

The American College of Neuropsychopharmacology,

which gained its initial impetus from the discovery of tranquilizers, is one of the most vigorous and productive organizations to grace the field of behavioral science in many generations. It fosters continuing communication and collaboration among scientists from many disciplines.

The pharmacological revolution has also produced important changes in the public image of psychiatry, and in the professional activities of practicing mental health specialists. Along with the growing interest of many psychological and social scientists in mental health, there has been an increasing number of therapists from nonmedical disciplines who claim that their therapeutic expertise rivals that of the trained psychiatrist. In response, the psychiatrist is slowly turning his attention to the biological area and to the interface between psychiatry and the rest of medicine. In a sense, the identity and security of the profession hang in the balance, for psychiatry cannot exist as a true profession if it does not possess unique and specialized knowledge and techniques.

Psychopharmacology, electrotherapy, psychosomatic medicine, liaison psychiatry, the management of brain damage cases, and the psychiatric complications and sequelae of neurological and medical disease attract young psychiatrists more than ever before. These are areas in which it would appear that the psychiatrist can claim skills and knowledge not easily acquired by nonphysicians. Thus, the somatic-pharmacological revolution has given the psychiatrist new strength and identity.

How pervasive is the effect of the pharmacological revolution? It touches all members of mental health teams: the psychologist, social worker, nurse, rehabilitation worker. It also influences the practices of neurologists, family practitioners, specialists in internal medicine, pediatricians, and many others. All professionals working with the mentally ill must master at least the rudiments of psychopharmacology;

and in particular, those who are privileged to prescribe medication must at the very least become experts in the drugs they prescribe.

This book takes the viewpoint of the practicing psycho-pharmacologist and clinician, but does not limit its scope to psychopharmacology alone. It derives its strength from the considerable clinical and research experience of Dr. Alberto DiMascio* and Dr. Harold Goldberg, both of whom have had a great deal of hospital and community responsibility for treatment of a wide variety of patients.

This book is remarkably up to date and may be studied with profit by all who are treating mentally ill patients and contributing to the upgrading of systems of mental health.

Milton Greenblatt, M.D.

*Dr. DiMascio's untimely death in 1978 removed from our midst a most effective and creative colleague, friend, and counselor.

Publisher's notes

Alberto DiMascio, Ph.D., was at the time of his death Director of Psychopharmacology for the Department of Mental Health, Commonwealth of Massachusetts.

Harold L. Goldberg, M.D., is Clinical Professor in Psychiatry at Tufts University School of Medicine and Director of the West-Ros-Park Mental Health Center, Boston.

Milton Greenblatt, M.D., who wrote the Foreword, is Professor and Executive Vice-Chairman of the Department of Psychiatry and Biobehavioral Sciences and Director of Neuropsychiatric Hospital and Clinics—both at the University of California, Los Angeles.

Much of the content of this book has been adapted from articles on the same topics written by the authors and published originally in *Current Prescribing* and *Hospital Physician* magazines.

Fred Witzig of Tenafly, N.J., designed the book.

Introduction

This book is designed as an aid to understanding and dealing with the most common psychiatric problems amenable to drug therapy. It is aimed at all those who must deal with these problems, from students in the helping professions to physicians, social workers, nurses, and related professions. Its focus on a simplified understanding of the major diagnostic considerations in each problem area and on the appropriate management of the problems found should allow it to be useful to the novice and the seasoned worker.

The book takes an eclectic approach to the accepted and customary practice of present-day psychiatry and psychopharmacology. Its guidelines reflect the experience of the authors and their collation of recommended practices from the literature. The book attempts to reflect the most current thinking on the selection of appropriate psychotropic medication, its hazards, dose scheduling, and duration of treatment.

On the basis of the authors' research, and their clinical teaching experience in hospitals and community-based patient-care programs, they espouse an eclectic approach—scientifically based, pragmatic, and reasonable.

The opening chapter on interviewing provides guidelines for approaching the patient, taking a history, and determining his mental status in an orderly and efficient manner. Understanding the parts of the mental-status examination, defining them, and differentiating them provide the building blocks on which the rest of the book is built.

An outline on acute schizophrenia covers the major considerations in the diagnosis and management of this disease, with primary and secondary symptoms presented. Management includes both psychosocial and somatic therapies, and the chapter concludes with recommended drug treatment, schedules, and effects.

Chronic schizophrenia is described according to the symptoms of both inherent and hospital-induced forms. The chapter explains the pharmacotherapy of the state, including aims, drug selection, maintenance, and hazards of long-term treatment. The guidelines for psychotherapy, rehabilitation, and resocialization provide the balance necessary to manage this complex problem.

Depression, a lethal psychiatric illness, is dealt with so as to help the reader be alert for suicidal issues and to seek the diagnosis of this disorder in areas that are often overlooked. Differential diagnosis of the various depressive illnesses is outlined, as are treatment approaches, including a guide to various drugs, with their respective advantages and disadvantages.

The chapter on mania focuses on the speed with which this problem can now be alleviated. Even more important, it clarifies the techniques of preventing this formerly troublesome disease.

The chapter on anxiety defines the problems, presenting symptoms, and treatment modalities. It explains the origins of symptoms and methods of dealing with them through psychotherapeutics.

The chapter on drugs in pregnancy focuses on the effects of medications: producing chromosomal breaks prior to conception; passing through the placental barrier and appearing in fetal blood; causing spontaneous abortions or premature births; affecting the labor, delivery, and the perinatal period; producing birth abnormalities; and appearing in the milk of nursing mothers.

Chapter 8 deals with the use of psychotropic drugs in children. It concentrates on three major groups of psychiatric problems: psychotic and psychoneurotic disorders, and minimal brain dysfunction.

The final phase of life, geriatrics, is the subject of the last chapter. It explores the problems, describes their manifestations, and concludes with their appropriate treatment. The various drugs administered to the elderly are classified, their relative merits examined, and complications of their use explored.

Thus this book covers a lifetime of problems and disorders. It moves from the prenatal problems caused by certain drugs through the problem of helping elderly people die gracefully and with dignity. Sandwiched between are some of man's most painful dilemmas, presented so that the reader may better understand them and more important, so he may provide less painful and more appropriate alternatives.

Alberto DiMascio, Ph.D.
Harold L. Goldberg, M.D.

1 Interviewing the psychiatric patient

1 Interviewing the psychiatric patient

To treat any psychiatric patient, a physician must gain a thorough knowledge of him, his problems, and his immediate environment. The primary means is the psychiatric examination. But no one can perform such an examination without creating at least a rudimentary rapport with his patient. The examiner should realize that no matter how crazy the patient's behavior may seem, he is a real person suffering from considerable pain, anguish, and fear—all of which affect his behavior and cause him to experience the world very differently from the way a normal individual does. To achieve rapport you must present yourself as a real person, who is:

— Offering help
— Willing to listen
— Able to set limits
— Not excessively frightened
— Not merely filling in forms
— Not trying to write down every word
— Willing to be confidential
— Not telling his own problems or stories
— Concerned with understanding the patient's problems and helping to solve them.

The interview may often be opened easily by merely saying, ''Why are you here?'' or ''What brings you to the clinic today?'' This may lead to a long dissertation, but it opens the way for the patient to describe in his own words what is going on.

To proceed successfully from this point, the interviewer should have a mental outline—or a written outline if he is a novice—of what material he needs to direct the interview. Certain basic data should be obtained and written down at the time of the interview. It is extremely important to record the interview carefully, so if someone else reads that record, he can get a good understanding of what the patient was like at the time and how the patient conceives of his life. The record should contain all pertinent clinical information so the reader can determine what the central conflict is.

Here is an outline of the psychiatric history:

I Identification

— Name, address, age, sex
— Ethnic or cultural background, marital status, occupation, religion
— Name of referral source, reason for referral, previous psychiatric treatment, date of examination

II Chief complaint (stated in patient's own words)

III History of present illness

Content

— List the patient's current problems, as he sees them, that cause him to seek help.
— Record events from his most recent stable state of functioning to present decompensation. ("When did you last feel everything was O.K.?")

Technique

— Record patient's own words insofar as possible, even though they may not seem to make sense.

4

— Make clear, chronological statements.
— Get information from others if patient is very young, psychotic, or senile.
— Identify informants (relative, friend), and use informants' own words.
— Don't use informants' information to cross-examine patient.

IV Past history

Approach

— Make this a statement of how the patient views what his life was like, not just a statement of historical fact.
— Include as much as possible of the patient's experience in his own words.
— Record salient events, not a rambling autobiography.
— Strive to understand how patient has responded to stress in his life.

Content of past history

— Childhood

Eating habits

Bowel habits and toilet training

Discipline

Sleep habits

Playmates

Unusual childhood illnesses or injuries

Reactions to starting school

School experiences and adjustment

Degree of academic success or failure

Truancy

5

Behavior problems

Physical and sexual development

General problems

— Adolescence

Age of onset of puberty

Menstrual history (females)

Friendship patterns

Dating patterns

Sexual experiences

Separation from family

Legal difficulties

Drug and alcohol experiences

— Adulthood

Educational and intellectual attainments

Occupational adjustment

Sexual adjustment

Attitudes toward sex

Courtship patterns

Marital adjustment

Military history

Religious attitudes

Hobbies

Ambitions and goals

v Family history

Content

— Inquire who makes up the current household (family

6

members, others); describe them by name, age, relationship—and write in the patient's words what they are like.

— Get a detailed description of the mother and father or other persons who raised the patient through childhood; to determine the early-life feeling tone between patient and parents, ask the patient to describe his earliest memory of each parent.

— Detail early relationships with parents and siblings: what the home life was like in reality and how the patient felt about it.

— Explore the patient's attitude toward his parents—and learn which he felt closer to—and their attitude toward him, and his reaction to their influence.

— Include family psychopathology, including arguments, alcoholism, separation, divorce, incarceration, and hospitalization.

— Ask how family members—parents, siblings, grandparents, depending on their roles in the family—reacted to death.

— Determine the family's psychiatric history: contacts with therapists, psychiatric hospitalizations, and most importantly, responses of family members. Investigate which therapies—such as electroshock and psychotropic drugs—have worked well for other members of the patient's family, because experience indicates that they will most likely work well for the patient, too. Ask about suicide: Suicide risk increases significantly for individuals whose relatives have successfully killed themselves; such circumstances seem to give permission to the patient, taking suicide out of the realm of something that "just is not done."

— Inquire about other family crises, such as frequent moves, house fires, and the like.

7

VI Medical and psychiatric history

Medical and surgical

Psychiatric

— Note psychiatric treatments, therapists, institutions, discharges, dates, and get permission to contact therapists. Explore the patient's attitudes toward former therapists.
— Determine which drugs have been prescribed and also reasons, responses, and side effects; find out which over-the-counter medicines and street drugs the patient has used. (Don't overlook amphetamines or other diet pills, which can cause amphetamine psychosis or mood changes on withdrawal.)
— Report drinking habits and estimate alcohol consumption; but remember that the rule of thumb is to double the figure that an alcoholic gives you.
— Evaluate suicide potential in alcoholics and drug addicts; the risk is greatest in adolescence and the involutional period after age 55.

VII Mental-status examination

General approach

The mental-status evaluation is perhaps the most important part of a psychiatric examination, allowing you to elicit specific evidence of mental-apparatus malfunctions, identify psychopathology, and discover disorders of thinking, mental functioning, affect, and orientation. The patient's condition and his response to the interview situation determine how deeply you can probe. When you deal with a relatively intact and normal person, it quickly becomes evident if the patient has difficulty in mental functioning. Thus it may not be necessary to go into a lengthy, formal mental-status examination with every patient, especially as you gain experience in interacting with patients. However, such an assessment is a valuable tool, especially if the examiner is a novice or student or if the patient is not well integrated. It is essential to make a written record of each examination, so you can substantiate changes in the patient.

Examiner's attitude

A patient quickly senses that an examiner considers the task routine and performs it perfunctorily. That feeling affects the validity of the results; the same is true if the examiner does not understand the purpose of the examination, is defensive about administering it, or is awkward. You should strive to obtain information on mental status during the general interview by following the patient's lead and asking questions at appropriate times.

Patient's condition

Even though thoroughness is important, you should keep in mind that you are dealing with sick people who may not be able to tolerate a complete examination at one sitting. And because of resistance or pathology, a patient may not cooperate fully. Be considerate: Treat the patient as you would like to be treated.

Specific items to record
— General appearance and behavior
   Dress
   Posture
   Facial expression
   Motor activity

Physical characteristics

Mood, as seen by the interviewer

Reaction to the interviewer (Is the patient hostile or obsequious? How does he make the interviewer feel?)

Mannerisms such as posturing, tics, agitation, hand wringing, pacing, or crying

— Speech

Quality: pronunciation, loudness, inflection, and continuity (halting, rapid, slow)

Quantity: pressure of speech, freedom, openness, and monosyllabic responses

Organization: logic, circumstances, flight of ideas, word salad, etc.

Disorders of speech: stuttering, scanning, slurring, or aphasia

— Emotional state and mood affect

Appropriateness of emotional responses

Disturbances in regulating emotions: Can the patient control his emotions?

Mood fluctuations: Does his mood change during the interview? ("What part of the day is most difficult or most pleasant?")

Appropriateness of affect: Is the affective display appropriate to the situation? Is it shallow or incongruous? Is the affect dull or flattened? Does the patient jest about sad events or weep over funny events?

Sociability: Is the patient introverted or isolated? Does he prefer to be alone?

Depression: Differentiate depression—deep and melancholic affect—from withdrawal affect—flat and dissociated. It is absolutely essential to inquire about suicidal tendencies; any clue should be followed up with more questions. ("Do you get sad?" "When you feel this way, does it seem that you can't go on?" "Have you ever thought of doing away with yourself?" "Have you made plans to do so?")

Elation

Feelings of unreality: Does the patient feel detached, in a dreamlike state? What brings this about?

Anger: Does he have fantasies of assault? Has he ever acted on them? How does he react while driving? Does he have a long record of traffic violations? Does he get into fights easily? Does he ever feel angry enough to kill? (Patients who seem homicidal often commit suicide and vice versa.)

— Thought

In eliciting details about content of thought, the examiner must employ special skill and reasonable control of his own anxiety about the material that may appear. Directness, if properly timed, or if combined with reassurance, need not be traumatic. The patient should not assume or sense that the examiner is beating around the bush because of his own anxiety or disapproval of the patient's symptoms, thoughts, or hallucinations. (Much of the material can be obtained during the general interview: the order of interview items serves merely as a guide.)

Production: flow of thoughts with reference to their acceleration or retardation

Continuity: clear, coherent, relevant, rambling,

blocked, persevering, circumstantial, marked by flight of ideas

Content

a. Compulsions (repetitive acts that the patient feels driven to do, such as handwashing and counting)

b. Obsessions (repetitive thoughts that enter the patient's mind beyond his control)

c. Ruminations (repetitive or continuous speculation, which is often circular and interferes with all other thought processes)

d. Doubting (indecision about what to wear, what to eat, what to do)

e. Phobic thoughts (irrational fears of crowds, heights, and the like)

f. Anxiety (tenseness, uptightness): Does it have an identifiable source?

g. Depersonalization (a loss of sense of identity): Does the patient feel different or changed?

h. Feelings or delusions of persecution: Are people hostile to the patient? Plotting against him? Poisoning him? Pursuing him? If so, why?

i. Feelings of influence: Is the patient being controlled or influenced?

j. Ideas of reference: Do people on TV talk directly to him? Do street lights shine in certain ways to deliver messages to him?

k. Somatic preoccupations and delusions (internal changes in the patient's bodily structure or function, often of a bizarre nature and frequently focused on digestion, elimination, or sex)

l. Delusions of grandeur ("Has God been very good to you?" "Can you communicate directly with God?" "Do you have any influential contacts or relatives?" "Are you in charge of many things?" "Can you control the world?")

m. Illusions (particularly important in delirious patients): Does the patient misinterpret sensory data? Are the patient's perceptions affected by conditions or time of day?

n. Hallucinations (subjective, false sensory perceptions in the absence of external stimuli): Often patients volunteer information regarding hallucinations, but sometimes only patients' behavior—such as responding to voices—reveals them. Hallucinations strongly suggest psychosis.

— Auditory hallucinations: They are most frequently experienced as voices; they may be threatening, accusing, obscene, terrifying, or reassuring.

— Visual hallucinations: They are less common than other kinds and occur most frequently as a symptom of toxic psychosis, as in drug overdose or delirium tremens. Patients may see images, scenes, the Lord's face, and various bizarre but very real elements.

— Tactile hallucinations (painful sensations, things crawling on skin, and the like)

o. Dreams: How often? How vivid? Are they repetitions or nightmares? What is the content?

p. Hypnagogic phenomena (dreamlike experiences occurring in twilight states between falling asleep and sleep and between sleep and waking up): It is important to differentiate them from true hallucinations, but hypnagogic phenomena do not represent pathology.

13

q. Déjà vu experiences (sensations of having been in a similar place or situation before): These, too, may be normal occurrences, but may also be the means of uncovering delusional thoughts.

— Somatic functioning

Range of physical symptoms

Appetite: change in appetite, interest in food

Bowel habits

Menstrual and sexual disturbances: changes in sexual appetite or activity, sexual identity

Sleep disturbances ("How quickly do you fall asleep?" "Do you sleep through the night?" "Do you awaken prematurely?" "How well rested do you feel on awakening?")

— Cognitive functions

Not every patient requires total cognitive testing. These tests are indicated for distinguishing between organic brain disease and functional psychogenic illness, diagnosing delirium and dementia, and estimating intelligence in patients who may seem mentally deficient.

It is particularly important to be aware of the patient's reaction to test questions, which he may interpret as threatening, humiliating, insulting, or annoying. Testing should be clearly explained so the patient can understand its purpose. One useful way is to explain test results as a baseline for checking progress and determining eventual recovery.

If the patient fails questions, do not give the correct answers; they may influence his performance on future examinations.

Orientation time, place, and identity. Does the patient recognize the identities of the people around him? Does he know the current date—day, month, and year? (It is very important to ask for the complete date; it is not unusual for a patient to know the correct month and day but believe that he is living in a different year from the present one.) How did the patient get to the hospital?

Attention and concentration

a. Digit span: The patient should be tested on his ability to repeat, both forward and backward, a series of digits read to him by an examiner. He should correctly repeat from five to eight digits forward and from four to six digits backward. It is unusual for a patient of any age to miss more than three digits forward and backward.

b. Calculation: Subtraction by sevens and simple addition or multiplication are tests of arithmetical ability and of concentration.

Memory

a. Recent memory (recall of events since hospitalization, food in last meal, home address, phone number, current events): Check the accuracy of some of these items to be sure that the patient is not confabulating (reciting imaginary experiences to fill memory gaps). The question "Have you seen me before?" may be quite helpful: A patient who confabulates often answers affirmatively, giving fabricated details of a prior meeting.

b. Remote memory: This is tested during the history; questions involving birthdate, age, and the like can be helpful.

15

Fund of information and vocabulary

If you have not sized up the patient on these points during the general history, ask a series of gradually more difficult questions. ("How many things are there in a dozen?" "How many pounds are there in a ton?" "How far is it from Boston to Los Angeles?" "What is the capital of Greece?") In a combined memory-and-information test, ask the patient to list the Presidents of the U.S., starting with the incumbent and going back as far as possible. Discuss current events; ask questions about noted politicians.

Abstract thinking

This is a particularly important aspect of the patient's intellectual functioning because it is vulnerable to organic pathology and thought impairment of schizophrenia. Two subjects are useful—proverbs and similarities. One test may be administered this way: "You know what a proverb is, don't you? A proverb is a saying. What do people mean when they say, _____?" Examples of proverbs you can use are: "People who live in glass houses shouldn't throw stones." "Don't count your chickens before they're hatched." "There's no use crying over spilled milk."

A patient, considering the first proverb, may start talking about breaking glass, houses, or picking up a stone—without getting into the abstract quality of the proverb. His thinking can be considered concrete. Patients may need further prompting—someone who initially gives a concrete response may be capable of abstracting.

16

Testing the capacity to discover similarities is a second approach. For example, ask, "How are a bird and an airplane alike?" "A plum and a peach?"

Judgment (general appreciation of social conventions): Ask questions like these: "What would you do if you found a stamped, addressed letter lying on the street?" "What would you do if you spotted a fire in a movie house?"

Perception, coordination, and visual motor functioning. Observe the patient writing or copying a circle, diamond, cross, or other shape drawn on paper. See if he is capable of doing so with reasonable speed and coordination.

Insight (the patient's awareness of how he behaves, how his behavior affects the community, whether it is bizarre or unrealistic, what the patient's attitude is toward his symptoms, and how he plans to act in the future).

VIII Psychodynamic formulation

At this point, the interviewer can put together conclusions drawn from the data, which state how the patient came to be the way he is and what theoretical, dynamic explanations account for his current situation. The interviewer gains a diagnostic impression of the patient's symptoms and the origins of his problems, as based on his history and character traits. The psychodynamic formulation is meant to be a summary and conclusion; therefore, no new information and data should be introduced during this phase.

17

The first half of each following chapter is structured so that an examiner may compare information obtained from patients to the interview outline of this chapter, to make an appropriate diagnosis. The second half of each chapter is devoted to treatment.

2 Diagnosing and treating acute schizophrenia

2 Diagnosing and treating acute schizophrenia

Acute schizophrenia takes a heavy toll in the United States. With an incidence of 0.5 to 1.0 per cent, it thus affects between 1,000,000 and 2,000,000 persons. Half of all hospitalized psychiatric patients (or one-fourth of all hospital patients) are acute schizophrenics. Despite the size of the problem, increasing numbers of patients are now able to function outside hospitals. Age of onset can be graphically represented by a bell-shaped distribution curve showing a peak for ages 16 through 24.

The disorder actually embraces a group of mental-disease processes. They are characterized by symptoms like unexpected emotional responses, thought defects (unusual thought content and conceptual disorganization), frequent delusions, and occasional hallucinations.

Symptoms

It is convenient to divide primary symptomology into four parts, or the "Four As," which serve as an aid to memory:

1. Affect. In schizophrenia, the patient's affect (feelings and emotions) appears to be separated from his thoughts. As a result, it is difficult to engage the patient in conversation; his interpersonal relationships are disturbed; and his thoughts may even be accompanied by inappropriate affect.

2. Associations. A schizophrenic links separate thoughts illogically. He may range from going off on a tangent to expressing totally irrelevant ideas.

3. Attention. A patient cannot focus on one thing at a time; he is preoccupied and distracted. Frequently an early symptom is the inability to concentrate.

4. Autism. As a schizophrenic loses his connections with reality, he contacts a substitute world instead. The patient may refer to events occurring in this substitute world. He loses his ability to abstract, and he may panic.

Secondary symptoms represent defenses or attempts at restitution. They dominate the clinical picture and may be organized into the following diagnostic categories:

Simple symptoms

    Apathy

    Indifference

    Emotional blunting or flatness

    Inability to make associations

    Impoverished interpersonal relations

    Intellectual dullness

Hebephrenic symptoms (in which regression serves as a defense)

    Disorganized thinking

    Shallow, inappropriate affect and bizarreness

    Unpredictable giggling, facial contortions, or hand gestures

    Silly, childlike behavior

Catatonic symptoms (in which denial serves as defense)

    Excitement

        Excessive, sometimes violent motor activity

Possible assaultiveness or destructiveness

Exhaustion and starvation

Withdrawal

Mutism

Stupor

Negativism (even including refusal to eat)

Waxy flexibility (limbs placed in certain positions remain in those same positions for a long time)

Posturing

Paranoid symptoms (in which projection serves as a defense, with the patient transferring something that occurs within himself to the outside world)

Delusions of persecution or grandeur (false beliefs)

Frequent hallucinations (false sensory perceptions, usually auditory)

Occasional excessive religiosity

Behavior consistent with patient's delusions, which may lead to hostility and aggressiveness

Schizophrenia/schizoaffective symptoms

Schizophrenic symptoms mixed with pronounced elation or depression

Treatment

Psychosocial therapies generally have limited roles in treating schizophrenic patients. For example, individual psychoanalysis has little or no value in dealing with the acute phase—regardless of the therapist's theoretical orientation. And individual psychotherapy isn't very useful, either, during the initial acute phase, whether applied as uncovering or supportive psychotherapy. That is because its goals are long-term restoration of interpersonal functioning and emotional stability.

In group therapy, patients meet in groups to explore each other's problems, problem causes, and methods of coping. This technique may assist patients in resocialization, provide them with supportive structures, and force them to interact with others in the postacute phase. Still another method is milieu therapy, which consists of manipulating patients' environments to alter interpersonal stresses and help them learn new coping methods.

With one exception, somatic therapies have fallen from favor in treatment of schizophrenia. Insulin-coma therapy was originally reserved for severe, treatment-resistant schizophrenics but was found to be of little value and is seldom used today. It must be applied with great precision and extreme caution. Electroconvulsive therapy (ECT) was initially introduced because Von Meduna believed—incorrectly—that an "antagonism" exists between epileptic seizures and schizophrenia. Camphor, pentylenetetrazol (Metrazol), and then ECT were used to induce seizures. ECT, too, is now considered to have little efficacy in treating schizophrenics. However, psychosurgery—prefrontal lobotomy and lobectomy—is still of some use in carefully selected, severely disturbed patients. The procedures are rarely used because it is possible to irreversibly disrupt patients' personalities.

By contrast, pharmacotherapy can bring about remission of symptoms in the majority of acute schizophrenic episodes. Psychotropic drugs are most effective in the more acute, affectively charged, disorganized states with rapid onsets. All antipsychotics are equally effective as antischizophrenics, against target symptoms like these:

24

Overactivity

Hostility

Hallucinations and delusions

Inappropriate expressions of emotion

Unusual and disorganized thinking

Insomnia

Poor self-care

Withdrawal

Grandiosity

Suspiciousness

Antipsychotic agents fall into five classes, according to their chemical structures:

● *Phenothiazines*. There are three chemical subclasses of phenothiazines: those with an aliphatic side chain produce a considerable degree of sedative-hypnotic, motor-inhibiting activity. They may also cause autonomic effects, hypotensive reactions, cardiovascular arrhythmias, hematologic and hepatic dysfunctions, and extrapyramidal effects (tremors, muscle rigidity, or muscle spasms). These latter effects may be treated by reducing phenothiazine dosage or giving antiparkinson medications. For clinical response, aliphatic phenothiazines must be administered in rather high doses, ranging from 400 to 1,000 mg daily. Representative of aliphatic phenothiazines are chlorpromazine (Thorazine) and triflupromazine hydrochloride (Vesprin).

Phenothiazines with a piperidine side chain are prescribed in lower doses to produce clinical response; dosage varies from 50 to 800 mg daily. In addition, they are less likely to provoke marked sedative-hypnotic effects, and the incidence of autonomic and extrapyramidal effects is low. Included among the piperidines are thioridazine hydrochloride (Mellaril), mesoridazine besylate (Serentil), and piperacetazine (Quide).

Phenothiazines with a piperazine side chain can be used in even smaller amounts, usually from 1 to 150 mg daily, depending on the specific drug. While seldom producing hypotension, they are likely to cause dystonic or dyskinetic side effects (spasmodic muscle contractions). Representing the piperazines are acetophenazine maleate (Tindal), butaperazine maleate (Repoise), carphenazine maleate (Proketazine), fluphenazine hydrochloride (Permitil, Prolixin), perphenazine (Trilafon), and trifluoperazine hydrochloride (Stelazine).

● *Thioxanthenes.* Though they are structurally similar to phenothiazines, the thioxanthenes do not produce the diversity or intensity of side effects that occur with their phenothiazine counterparts. Thioxanthenes are much less likely to bring on cardiovascular disruptions or hematologic and hepatic dysfunctions. The sole aliphatic thioxanthene available in the United States is chlorprothixene (Taractan), and the only piperazine thioxanthene is thiothixene (Navane).

● *Butyrophenones.* Most drugs of this class are currently unavailable in this country. They are highly potent in a range of 1 to 100 mg daily, and they reduce psychotic manifestations without sedative-hypnotic action. They rarely produce autonomic, cardiovascular, hematologic, or hepatic changes, and seldom interact with other drugs—in contrast to phenothiazines and thioxanthenes. However, they are the most likely of the group to cause dystonic or dyskinetic extrapyramidal side effects. Haloperidol (Haldol) is the prototype of the butyrophenones. Given intramuscularly, haloperidol can be useful for rapid treatment of acute psychosis.

• *Dibenzoxazepines.* A recently introduced drug with a chemical structure quite dissimilar from the above three is loxapine succinate (Loxitane). In the acute stages the drug is used in doses of 50-250 mg/day. In its clinical actions and side effects it is similar to the piperazine phenothiazines or thioxanthene. The major adverse reaction associated with it are extrapyramidal side effects.

• *Dihydroindolones.* Another recently introduced class of antipsychotics with a dissimilar chemical structure from any of the above is molindone hydrochloride (Moban). Generally, the dose in acute patients is 40-200 mg/day. A unique quality of this drug is the lack of weight gain often associated with a number of the above drugs. The major adverse reaction associated with it are extrapyramidal side effects.

There is no evidence that one class of antipsychotic agents is better than another for particular types of psychotic patients.

Drug treatment principles

1. Use only one drug at a time. There is no rational basis for combining antipsychotic drugs.

2. Initiate a drug on a q.d. or b.i.d. basis. On a b.i.d. schedule, prescribe one-third for the morning and two-thirds h.s. Pharmacologically, all psychotropic drugs are long-acting; only in severely agitated patients is more frequent dosage required for sedative, motor-inhibiting purposes. Patients who are physically healthy tolerate q.d. or b.i.d. schedules with fewer side effects than occur

if the drugs are administered more frequently.

3. Use a drug aggressively. Do not underdose. Raise dosage as rapidly as the patient can tolerate it (about every three to four days) until either the desired clinical response or markedly adverse effects are apparent.

4. If no clinical response has occurred after three to four weeks of treatment, one should consider switching to another subclass or class of drugs. Make sure dosage has been raised to a maximum before doing so.

5. Add antiparkinson drugs only after the patient develops extrapyramidal side effects. Do not use them before symptoms develop: These agents are of little value prophylactically. Besides, antiparkinson drugs are potent anticholinergic agents and can produce side effects that are additive to those produced by the antipsychotics.

6. Discontinue giving antiparkinson drugs for drug-induced extrapyramidal side effects after three to four months. Even if the antipsychotic drug is continued, 90 percent of withdrawn patients will not develop those side effects again.

7. Adjust dosage to allow for route of administration. Parenterally administered antipsychotics are three to four times more potent than the same drugs given orally.

8. Query a patient about his family's responses to drugs. A positive or negative history of experience with a given drug augurs a corresponding response in the patient.

9. Do not withdraw an antipsychotic too soon. Remember that a patient who has had an acute schizophrenic episode generally needs maintenance pharmacotherapy for a long period—at least two to four months after symp-

toms are controlled. The maintenance dose should be kept at the lowest level that will insure improvement. The approximate daily range is 200 to 500 mg of chlorpromazine (Thorazine) or the equivalent of another drug. Below this level, a drug will be of little value; above it, there is danger of overmedication.

10. Know the drugs you are using! If you must prescribe more than one medication to treat diverse physical or mental symptomatology, remember that concomitant multiple drug use can lead to a variety of adverse drug interactions. Psychotropics react with other psychotropics and with many other kinds of medication.

Table 2-1

Drug dosages in acute-phase schizophrenia

Chemical class	Commonly used drug	Daily dosage range (mg)
Phenothiazines	Chlorpromazine (Thorazine)	600-1,000
	Thioridazine hydrochloride (Mellaril)	600-800
	Perphenazine (Trilafon)	32-48
	Trifluoperazine hydrochloride (Stelazine)	30-40
	Fluphenazine hydrochloride (Permitil, Prolixin)	10-20
	Fluphenazine decanoate (Prolixin Decanoate)	27-75 (1-3 cc) every 2-3 weeks
	Fluphenazine enanthate (Prolixin Enanthate)	25-75 (1-3 cc) every 2-3 weeks
Thioxanthenes	Thiothixene (Navane)	30-50
	Chlorprothixene (Taractan)	200-600
Butyrophenones	Haloperidol (Haldol)	30-50
Dibenzoxazepines	Loxapine succinate (Loxitane)	50-250
Dihydroindolones	Molindone (Moban)	40-200

Suggested reading

Arieti, S., ed. *American Handbook of Psychiatry*. (3 vols). New York: Basic Books, 1959 & 1966.

DiMascio, A., and Shader, R., eds. *Clinical Handbook of Psychopharmacology*. New York: Science House, 1970.

Hollister, L. *Clinical Use of Psychotropic Drugs*. Springfield, Ill: Charles C Thomas, 1973.

3 Diagnosing and treating chronic schizophrenia

3 Diagnosing and treating chronic schizophrenia

Twenty-five to 30 percent of schizophrenic patients fail to recover from one or more acute episodes. They retain chronic personality defects, which apparently show acceptance of their illness (stable chronicity). The symptoms don't visibly disturb the patient, who often lacks spontaneity and often displays bizarre or stereotyped behavior. Many such patients live in this chronic state of incapacitation, with active signs of psychotic disability, for years. And these are the patients most conspicuous on the street, in clinics, and in private physicians' offices.

But in terminal deterioration, a patient's behavior becomes more impulsive or reflexlike. Hoarding of objects is replaced by food grabbing, and later by ingestion of small edible or inedible objects. In this stage, apparent somatosensory alterations take place: Although patients still react to olfactory stimuli, they seem insensitive to taste sensations, pain, heat, and cold. This anesthesia is the cause of many accidents, for example, when a patient is burned by sitting too close to a radiator.[1]

Symptomatology

Symptoms noted in chronic schizophrenics may result from the disease itself, such as those typically seen in patients residing in the community who have had no history of long-term hospitalization. In addition, some symptoms may arise from long-term institutionalization, which induces specific new syndromes.

Chronic schizophrenics in the community are marked by residual symptomatology. Primary symptoms are flat

affect, inability to make associations, distracted attention, autistic thoughts, and ambivalence, while secondary
symptoms include regression, projection, disorganization, bizarreness, gesturing, withdrawal, negativism, delusions, and hallucinations. Not being completely alleviated, they lead to inappropriate behavior:

- A patient's dress may be bizarre, untidy, or inappropriate for weather conditions.

- A patient's mannerisms and ritualistic behavior may
take the form of posturing, repeated facial grimaces
and tics, compulsive touching of objects, pacing, repeated shouts, or movements of the limbs; he persists
in this behavior even when it annoys others or causes
them to stare at the patient.

- A patient responds to hallucinations by conversing
with a hallucinated voice, shouting epithets at a non-
existent person, and by shifting his attention from
work or conversation to hallucinated material.

- A patient shows excessive suspicion and paranoia; he
may become totally unable to trust others, hostile
without provocation, and afraid of being poisoned by
food or medication—and may feel that people are
looking at him or talking about him.

- A patient displays grandiosity, a feeling of superpow-
er, with delusions that cause him to be excessively
suspicious; in fact, he may sense that he is the Mes-
siah, an agent of God or the devil, or a great political
leader.

- A patient develops inappropriate emotional responses: He reacts unpredictably to everyday problems and so becomes unreliable.

In hospitalization-induced symptomatology—sometimes called the "institutionalization syndrome"—the patient's basic symptoms are accentuated and specific new changes are added:

- A patient undergoes motivational decline because large state hospitals too often serve as warehouses for chronically ill patients rather than as treatment facilities; a patient grows progressively more apathetic and indifferent.

- A patient shows increased flatness of affect—a natural result of the institution's failure to stimulate him; he interacts with others in only very basic, automatonlike activities that further impoverish affect.

- A patient becomes isolated from his family and peer groups and lowers his social standards if unacceptable behavior is tolerated by the staff of the institution.

- A patient loses coping and decision-making skills as institutional life forces dependency on the institution; his rhythm of life deteriorates to just meeting his basic biological needs: eating, drinking, eliminating, and sleeping.

- A patient loses productive vocational skills when he no longer needs to produce in a meaningful way; available institutional jobs usually cannot be translated into jobs in the community, and lack of the usual rewards makes it as easy not to work as to work.

- A patient may be abandoned by his family and society: The family of a chronically institutionalized patient gradually comes to deny the patient's very existence and may not visit him for years on end. And

37

citizens object if attempts are made to move him and other chronic patients into community residences.

- A patient fails to advance educationally; he suffers a decline in motivation, as the institution neglects academic or vocational pursuits.

Pharmacotherapy

Available antipsychotics, which are equally effective in the management or maintenance treatment of chronic schizophrenia, fall into five major chemical classes:

1. Phenothiazines

— Aliphatic phenothiazines, represented by chlorpromazine (Thorazine) and triflupromazine hydrochloride (Vesprin)
— Piperedine phenothiazines, represented by thioridazine hydrochloride (Mellaril), mesoridazine besylate (Serentil), and piperacetazine (Quide)
— Piperazine phenothiazines, represented by acetophenazine maleate (Tindal), butaperazine maleate (Repoise), carphenazine maleate (Proketazine), fluphenazine hydrochloride (Permitil, Prolixin), perphenazine (Trilafon), and trifluoperazine hydrochloride (Stelazine)

2. Thioxanthenes

— Aliphatic thioxanthenes, the sole available drug in the U.S. being chlorprothixene (Taractan)
— Piperazine thioxanthenes, the sole available drug in the U.S. being thiothixene (Navane)

3. Butyrophenones

— Haloperidol (Haldol) is the sole available butyrophenone in the U.S. for use in the treatment of chronic schizophrenia.

4. Dibenzoxazepines

— The sole available drug in this class is loxapine succinate (Loxitane).

5. Dihydroindolones

— The sole available drug in this class is molindone hydrochloride (Moban).

Most of these medications for chronic schizophrenia are available in a variety of forms—tablets, concentrates, or injectables—but only fluphenazine is also available in preparations providing an extended period of pharmacological or clinical activity. Fluphenazine enanthate (Prolixin Enanthate) and fluphenazine decanoate (Prolixin Decanoate) are injectables with a two- to three-week duration of activity.

Two major aims of maintenance treatment with antipsychotics are sustaining the degree of symptom reduction or behavior modification achieved during the acute phase treatment, and preventing relapse. Seldom is medication continued in the hope of alleviating symptoms completely.

Generally speaking, the most effective antipsychotic for a patient during his acute phase is also the most likely drug to be selected for his maintenance treatment. Another rationale for selecting a drug is to avoid drugs that can produce adverse effects when given over a long period or with dosage accumulation. Examples are dermatologic, ocular, or cardiac-muscle pigmentation, and persistent dyskinesia, which are described later in this chapter.

Some patients refuse to take medications when they

notice symptoms abating and are discharged from the hospital. Then they may relapse and have to return to the institution. For such patients, fluphenazine enanthate or decanoate may be of value since this form of medication assures that the patient is receiving the drug.

Dosage in the maintenance phase is reduced to the lowest level that prevents recurrence of symptoms. This level is one-half to one-third the dose given in the acute-treatment phase. Undermedicating is as unsound as over-medicating. The best clinical and pharmacologic evidence favors a dosage range of 200 to 500 mg of chlor-promazine, or its equivalent, for maintenance therapy.

Some patients require maintenance therapy for the rest of their lives. Others, after a time, may be discontin-ued without showing a return of symptoms. There is no sound basis for predicting which course the patient may take. Indeed, there is only one way to tell if a patient requires the medication: Discontinue it and watch him for signs of relapse. One should not only be on the lookout for a continuing need for the medication, but also evalu-ate objective evidence of any beneficial response to it that occurred when the patient was taking the medication.

Good-risk candidates for drug discontinuation are younger patients who have experienced their first epi-sodes, had illnesses of short duration, had good premor-bid histories, and exhibited considerable affect during their illnesses. Patients who have been on inadequate doses of psychotropic drugs—that is, less than 200 mg of chlorpromazine or its equivalent—are good discontinua-tion risks, too. But if symptoms reappear, patients should immediately be given their prior medications. Patients show a decreased risk of relapse after two consecutive drug-free years.

Psychotropic drugs and their metabolites are stored in

body tissues and only slowly released. When the medications are discontinued, most patients who have been on them for more than six months do not show a return of symptoms for one or two months. This is the crucial time to observe a patient closely for symptomatology requiring medication to avert a full-blown relapse.

Even in patients on lifetime maintenance therapy, intermittent treatment is a good policy for avoiding hazards. Intermittent treatment is drug discontinuation once a year. It should be tried in patients who seem relatively stabilized and asymptomatic.

The hazards of long-term psychotropic medication can be conveniently classified:

I Ocular effects

— Bilateral, symmetrical pigmentary deposits in the central portions of the anterior lens capsules (stellate configuration) with chlorpromazine, thioridazine, and thiothixene

a. These deposits produce little or no impairment of visual acuity.

b. Such effects generally disappear with discontinuation of medication, but they can remain for years.

c. Yearly slit-lamp examinations provide the only method of detection.

— Epithelial keratopathy that is confined to the exposed cornea

a. White, gray, and brown opacities of linear, curvilinear, or spiral formations occur.

b. Keratopathy does not impair patient's visual acuity

41

and improves rapidly after medication is discontinued.

— Cataract formation in rare instances

II Dermatologic effects, with pigmentation of skin varying from slate gray to metallic purple

— Confined to portions of the body exposed to sunlight.
— Occur with phenothiazines and thioxanthenes.
— Disappear with drug discontinuation.

III Cardiovascular effects

— ECG changes—such as T-wave depression or notching, QT interval prolongation, and increasing convexity of ST segment—which are produced by aliphatic and piperidine phenothiazines and are readily reversible on drug discontinuation
— Ventricular arrhythmia and tachycardia
— Pigmentary deposits in myocardium and arterioles noted in cases of sudden myocardial failure
— Decrease in stroke volume, fall in arterial blood pressure, and decreased cardiac output during exercise—which may limit physical performance and may occur after high-dose, long-term treatment with the aliphatic phenothiazines

IV Neurological effects

— Extrapyramidal symptoms (which sometimes result when patients are maintained on large doses of antipsychotic drugs)

a. Tremor, stiffness, and altered gait resembling naturally occurring paralysis agitans

b. Uncontrollable restlessness, known as akathisia

— Tardive dyskinesia

a. It is so called because it is noted late in the course of treatment, usually after a year of continuous treatment and is also termed persistent dyskinesia, because the symptoms are untreatable and persist for long periods.

b. Caused especially by phenothiazines, this condition may be masked by continued administration of the phenothiazines and may not be detected until after medication has been stopped. Its occurrence has led to a reappraisal of the value of uninterrupted and indefinitely prolonged antipsychotic drug therapy.

c. Signs consist of lingual-facial hyperkinesia, chewing motions, tongue protrusion, choreoathetoid movements of extremities, or pill-rolling motions.

d. There is no known treatment; antiparkinson drugs do not help.

e. On noting first signs of the syndrome, a physician should discontinue the medication and not restart it. If the patient needs an antipsychotic, the physician may consider switching to haloperidol or the thioxanthenes, which may be less likely to produce the syndrome.

V Miscellaneous effects

— Galactorrhea, alone or accompanied by amenorrhea
— Chronic constipation, dilation of the intestine; and megacolon
— Weight gain, possibly related to hyperglycemic effects of long-term, high-dose phenothiazines

Psychotherapy

In psychotherapeutic management, the emphasis should

be on reality therapy rather than on classic insight therapy.[2] With a one-to-one approach, the goal is to promote improved object relations. Many management techniques are also applicable to chronic patients in their homes, where family involvement is forced and community supports are maintained.

The most important aim in family therapy is to prevent extrusion—the process by which a family member is identified as "sick" and gotten rid of by putting him away in the hospital. The entire family is seen and treated, not just the patient. This reinforces the concept that the illness is not purely the patient's problem, but one that the entire family plays a part in and must learn to cope with. So it is highly desirable for the patient to remain at home as a member of his family.

The community visiting nurse plays a key role in psychotherapeutic management as a therapist and observer, and in administering medication. Her accepted role of regular home visitor and medicator allows her easy access, as well as regular and continued follow-up. She is able to observe progress, medication side effects, crises, and other changes. She can call in a mobile crisis team or a home-treatment service from her local mental health center, so that rapid and early intervention can be made. Because the chronic form of the disease is lifelong, intermittent intervention by a mental-health specialty team is much more practical and economical than continued direct care in an institution.

As part of the acculturation process, ex-patients should have opportunities to meet people who accept them and supply them with necessary social supports, despite the stigma that is often associated with mental illness. The patient's resocialization is a learning and relearning of culturally acceptable personal and interper-

44

sonal behavior. The patient must learn to live with himself and others.[3]

Remotivation counseling for hospitalized patients is often tied to therapeutic maneuvers using behavior modification techniques based on Skinnerian learning principles. In the practical step system, patients move up a ladder of increasing privileges as they improve in taking on work responsibilities. The step system may be part of an imposed token economy: Patients receive tokens or cashable credits for all positive activity and lose them for negative behavior. This very direct reward-punishment model serves as an oversimplification of life, providing stepping-stones back to the real world. For patients in the community, the remotivation task is usually focused on getting the patient back into the mainstream of life, to encourage a return to school or work, and to nudge him out of his niche of fear and indifference.

Participating in the token economy and step system, patients can be resocialized—that is, taught to take pride in their appearance, behavior, work, and the like. They can relearn personal care and begin to throw off the chains of institutional dependence. Expatient clubs allow patients to begin social activities. Teaching life skills to formerly institutionalized patients is basic to accomplishing de-institutionalization. They must relearn how to shop, bank, ride buses and subways, find work, and get along in groups.

Day-care centers serve clinic and convalescent patients, including patients recently discharged from full-time hospitalization. The purpose of such partial freedom from hospitalization is to keep each patient as much as possible in his natural environment, where he continues to deal with personal social realities. By this means the patient continues to deal with familiar persons in the community: his personal physician, dentist, lawyer, and others. Even patients whose treatment may seem permanently custodial, with no end of partial hospitalization, can avoid the deterioration associated with full-time institutionalization. Their postdischarge treatment may include informal contacts through afternoon coffee hours and similar social functions. A so-called night hospital allows a patient to work days but to return to the hospital in the evening and stay until morning, an arrangement that provides transition but maintains hospital support. Foster homes, too, provide interaction, stimulation, and a supervised homelike atmosphere.

Halfway houses provide temporary shelter for posthospitalized patients before they establish independent residences. There patients share the common experience of having been hospitalized for mental illness. The sheltered social environment provides tolerance for behavior considered deviant elsewhere. Vocational assistance is a major function.

And then there are cooperative apartments or board-and-care facilities, which provide supervised group-living arrangements, where patients may move further toward the real world. They cook their own meals and care for their life-spaces while working days or visiting the day center.

Community residences are a blend of elements. Patients live in a supervised setting, prepare meals, care for their residence, and work toward life in the noninstitutional world outside.

Located in rural areas, work camps generally draw most of their patients from communities rather than hospitals. Emphasizing work therapy rather than vocational assistance, the camps also provide milieu treatment in a nonmedical environment.

46

Another form of work rehabilitation originates in ex-patient organizations, such as Fountain House in New York City, which provides work in private industry. Permanent positions in normal work settings are reserved for ex-patients; the club insures that some patients always cover the positions. And sheltered workshops, in or out of hospital, give patients work experience and allow them to relearn work habits, in settings that tolerate their idiosyncratic behavior. These two forms of work rehabilitation are often linked so that patients can move from the sheltered workshop to a normal work setting.

Table 3-1

Suggestions for long-term drug therapy in schizophrenia

---

1. Avoid polypharmacy with psychotropic drugs. Using two or more drugs provides no greater benefit than one antipsychotic—and there is a possibility of drug interactions with more than one.

---

2. Do not continue use of antiparkinson agents for more than three to four months. There is seldom any need to do so.

---

3. Administer medications b.i.d. or once a day h.s.

---

4. Give patient drug-free weekends. Drug or metabolites in tissues are released and recirculated during this period, so that a patient's behavior should remain under control.

---

5. Try periodically to discontinue drugs altogether, to determine if a patient still needs medication and to allow his body tissues to eliminate these ''toxic'' substances. This discontinuation may also aid in detecting early signs of tardive dyskinesia.

---

6. Give each patient a periodic (yearly) physical examination, including a slit-lamp examination and an ECG, if the patient remains on same drug regimen for a protracted period.

---

7. Consider switching to a new class or subclass of antipsychotics if patient's mental and behavioral status has remained steady—even though some residual symptoms remain and the current antipsychotic has been given continuously for a long time. The switch may result in further improvement.

Table 3-2

Drug-maintenance dosages
in chronic schizophrenia

Chemical class	Commonly used drug	Daily dosage range (mg)
Phenothiazines	Chlorpromazine (Thorazine)	200-500
	Thioridazine HCl (Mellaril)	200-400
	Perphenazine (Trilafon)	16-32
	Trifluoperazine HCl (Stelazine)	15-30
	Fluphenazine HCl (Permitil, Prolixin)	5-10
	Fluphenazine decanoate (Prolixin Decanoate)	12½-50 (½-2cc) every 2-3 wk
	Fluphenazine enanthate (Prolixin Enanthate)	12½-50 (½-2cc) every 2-3 wk
Thioxanthenes	Thiothixene (Navane)	20-40
	Chlorprothixene (Taractan)	100-400
Butyrophenones	Haloperidol (Haldol)	15-30
Dibenzoxazepines	Loxapine succinate (Loxitan)	50-200
Dihydroindolones	Molindone (Moban)	40-160

References

1. Arieti, S., ed. *American Handbook of Psychiatry*. (3 vols). New York: Basic Books, 1959 & 1966.

2. May, P. *Treatment of Schizophrenia*. New York: Science House, 1968.

3. Landy, D. Rehabilitation as a Sociocultural Process. *J Soc Issues* 16:3 1960.

4 Diagnosing and treating neurotic and psychotic depression

4 Diagnosing and treating neurotic and psychotic depression

Eight million people per year suffer from a depression severe enough to warrant treatment; 10,000,000 to 12,000,000 more need treatment but do not seek it. Three times as many females as males present with depression.

Depression is one of the few psychiatric illnesses with a significant mortality rate. There are approximately 40,000 known suicides annually from all causes in the United States. One expert has estimated that 2,000,000 persons make at least one attempt at self-destruction each year; clinical depression is present in at least half these cases.

Except for those with severe suicidal drives, most patients can be rapidly treated on an ambulatory basis, and the prognosis for acute depressive episodes is good. Half the patients, however, experience recurrences late in their lives, and 15 percent suffer from chronic illness, with continued low-grade depressive affect.

Depressive signs and symptoms

The characteristics of depression are numerous:

A. Exaggerated and persistent feelings of sadness, apathy, and loneliness

B. Pessimism and hopelessness, which help to differentiate depression from a normal, passing mood of sadness

C. Helplessness

D. Guilt and self-reproach: a patient's tendency to blame himself for his problems and even for others' difficulties, that may reach delusional levels

E. Motor-activity changes

— Retardation, with slowed speech, movement, and activity that may reach stuporous proportions
— Agitation: playing with hands and hair, hand wringing, nail biting, and hair pulling

F. Vegetative symptoms

— Fatigue: loss of energy, heaviness in limbs, inability to work, and difficulty in concentrating
— Loss of appetite
— Weight loss or gain
— Sleep disturbances: difficulty in falling asleep, restless sleep, early-morning awakening, and failure to feel rested after sleep
— Loss of interest in sex, which may lead to sexual dysfunctions such as impotence and orgasmic dysfunction—sometimes complicated by promiscuity as a patient tries to boost his ego
— Menstrual disturbances, usually amenorrhea
— Constipation
— Physiologic disturbances: increased sweating, tachycardia, pupillary dilatation, striated muscle spasms, and perceived pain of psychogenic origin

G. Suicide ideation and attempts

Suicide ideation, from the last-named category of depression characteristics, may vary from a simple wish to not wake up from sleep to detailed planning of suicide methods. Activity may range from unconsciously allowing accidents to occur through gestures of different sorts. Patients may make minor attempts, notify others of their attempts, or attempt suicide seriously.

Suicidal intent is rarely discovered without specifical-
ly asking about it! A physician does *not* precipitate suicide by asking about it and talking about it. In fact,
physicians should be more active in preventing suicide,
by watching for patients' loss of interest in themselves,
isolation from others, and preoccupation with self-destruction. Previous attempts are a very dangerous sign.
One study indicates that 72 percent of 50 suicides saw
their family physicians within three months of their
deaths and 62 percent within 30 days.

His family's predilection to suicide increases a patient's risk. So a family history should be elicited from
both patient and relatives, because such information is
rarely volunteered. Moreover, adolescent suicides are on
the increase. Adolescence is a time of impulsive activity,
and an adolescent's personality strengths and weaknesses
must be assessed. Conditions predisposing a young person to suicide include:

- Escape behavior, such as running away or using
  drugs

- An unwanted pregnancy

- Rejection by a boyfriend or girlfriend

- Seemingly trivial disappointments—flunking a
  course, not making a team—experienced by a susceptible individual

The varieties of depression

Depressive illnesses can be readily classified:

In psychotic depression, a patient's impaired mental
function interferes grossly with his capacity to meet the

55

demands of life. This may result from distorted recognition of reality or from distorted perceptions caused by delusions. Alterations of mood may impair the patient's capacity to respond appropriately. Deficits in perception, language, and memory may cause him to lose mental grasp of his situation. Spontaneous recovery seldom occurs, and active treatment must be given for extended periods. Temporary hospitalization is often necessary during the acute phase.

In neurotic depression, there is no gross misrepresentation of reality or gross personality disorganization. The patient is usually aware of his disturbed mental functioning, and mood disturbance usually does not pervade all aspects of his life. Spontaneous recovery occurs frequently, and the natural course of the illness spans five to 10 weeks. Even in the acute phase, the depressive is usually treated as an outpatient.

In masked depression, the illness often presents with symptoms suggesting physical disease or accompanying physical illness; in fact, physical symptoms may be major complaints. Physical diseases may also produce depressive symptoms directly through interference with central-nervous-system functioning.

Certain somatic diseases are more likely to lead to depression than others, particularly when they are serious and incapacitating and they require hospital care. Among these are malignancies, certain endocrine disorders (Cushing's syndrome and Addison's disease, for example), anemias, severe infections, asthma, rheumatoid arthritis, and ulcerative colitis. Such depression is a nonspecific psychological response to the stress of illness. Treatment of the physical illness may lift depression without psychotropic medications.

Attempts to treat physical illness, whether successful

or not, may sometimes uncover depression. Furthermore, some drugs—reserpine (Lemiserp, Rau-Sed, Resercen) and anovulatory drugs—may produce depression as a side effect. Either way, active treatment of the depressive symptoms is usually required, though discontinuation of the medication may be enough to reverse the depression. The oral-contraceptive-induced depression can be reversed by pyridoxine hydrochloride, 25 mg daily.

Differentiating depressions

A psychotic depressive reaction can be distinguished from a depressed-type manic-depressive illness because the former lacks a history of repeated episodes of depression or cyclothymic mood swings (including mania and hypomania) and also lacks periodicity of episodes. With a psychotic depressive reaction, there is also occasional evidence of specific precipitating stresses. Nonetheless, treatments for both kinds of illness are similar.

A psychotic depressive reaction is different from the schizoaffective-type, depressed schizophrenia, in that the latter is predominantly characterized by schizophrenic symptoms mixed with depressed-mood disturbances. The schizophrenic symptoms dominate the clinical picture more and more as the illness progresses. Therefore, the schizoaffective-type, depressed schizophrenia calls for the use of antipsychotics like a combination of perphenazine and amitriptyline hydrochloride (Etrafon, Triavil) or thioridazine hydrochloride (Mellaril). But such medication is not suitable for a psychotic depressive reaction.

A neurotic depression can be differentiated from an anxiety neurosis with depression because depressive affect is clearly more intense in the first, while anxiety symptoms are more conspicuous in the second. However,

57

depression and anxiety rarely exist separately, and both can usually be discovered, in varying degrees, in emotionally disturbed people. If depressive affect intensifies so that it is difficult to determine which symptom is more prominent, then that state is symptomatically labeled an anxious depression. In such cases, diazepam (Valium) may be a useful agent.

Pharmacotherapy

The first step in the pharmacotherapy of depression is to collect essential information. A comprehensive treatment history should be obtained, because a patient's previous drug responses are usually reliable guides to drug selection, dosages, and side effects. Furthermore, responses to psychoactive drugs are frequently similar among blood relatives. Indeed, familial experience with a particular drug is probably the best guide to choosing a drug for the depressed patient. So obtaining a family drug history is as important as learning how the patient himself reacts to medications.

A total drug profile should be obtained that includes drug regimens, objective and subjective responses, and side effects. This information prevents harmful drug interactions. An often overlooked factor is concurrent visits to other doctors. It is a common practice for patients to consult other physicians about drug side effects, because they do not realize what they are experiencing. You should remember that patients often self-medicate with proprietary products as well.

In tailoring drugs to patients' needs, drug actions are essential considerations. For instances, the tricyclics differ little from monoamine oxidase (MAO) inhibitors in speed of onset. The tricyclics are equal to MAO inhibitors clinically—or are even more effective—and have considerably less toxic potential.

Further, amitriptyline hydrochloride (Elavil), doxepin hydrochloride (Adapin, Sinequan), or imipramine hydrochloride (Presamine, Tofranil) have marked sedative-hypnotic and motor-inhibiting properties. On the other hand, phenelzine sulfate (Nardil), isocarboxazid (Marplan), tranylcypromine sulfate (Parnate), protriptyline hydrochloride (Vivactil), and desipramine hydrochloride (Norpramin, Pertofrane) have some stimulantlike actions. Doxepin and amitriptyline are the most effective anxiolytic agents, while drugs with stimulantlike actions may increase anxiety.

Selection of antidepressants should be made to utilize or avoid side effects, taking into account total symptomatology and specific properties of the antidepressants. For example, drug-induced drowsiness and psychomotor inhibition are clinically beneficial to an agitated patient with insomnia, but undesirable for an anergic patient complaining of fatigue. Doxepin or amitriptyline may be efficacious in a depressed patient with marked anxiety, while the MAO inhibitors or protriptyline may benefit a depressed patient who is atypical or anergic.

For agitated, hostile patients, thioridazine hydrochloride (Mellaril) has been reported to be effective. Diazepam (Valium) has been found to be of some use in anxious neurotic depressions but not of value in psychotic or hostile depressions. Finally, a combination of perphenazine and amitriptyline hydrochloride (Etrafon, Triavil) has been found to be effective in the treatment of schizo-affective-type, depressed schizophrenic patients.

An antidepressant should be used aggressively, starting with an effective dose level and increasing dosage every two to three days until clinical improvement is apparent or adverse reactions become intolerable. All tri-cyclic antidepressants can be given once a day at bedtime to physically healthy patients. Such a schedule has these advantages:

- It reduces complaints of side effects.

- It avoids need for bedtime sedatives.

- Its convenience improves compliance.

- It costs less.

Effects of medication

Signs of beneficial clinical change should be observed within a week in acutely ill, neurotically depressed patients whose illness is of less than two months' duration. Major improvements should take place within three to four weeks. In acute depressions of psychotic propor-tions, however, it may be two weeks before a physician can observe any reduction of symptoms, and major im-provement may require four to six weeks.

If a patient doesn't benefit clinically within these pe-riods, consider another tricyclic, one of the MAO inhibi-tors, or electroconvulsive therapy (ECT). Do not add another antidepressant; there is no advantage in combin-ing such drugs.

If clinical response occurs, continue the patient on an optimum dose for three months after resolution of depres-sive symptoms. Then switch to maintenance treatment: Two-thirds to one-half optimum level is suggested for an additional four to six months. Do not discontinue medica-tion too soon or too rapidly, because a relapse may occur.

The side effects of tricyclics include the following (though the first six rarely occur with doxepin):

Urinary hesitancy
Visual accommodation difficulties
Constipation
ECG irregularities
Orthostatic hypotension
Blockage of guanethidine hypotensive activity in hypertensive patients
Aggravation of narrow-angle glaucoma
Drowsiness
Increased sweating
Fine tremor of extremities

MAO inhibitors may produce these effects:

Restlessness
Agitation
Hyperreflexia
Hepatocellular damage
Maculopapular rashes
Insomnia
Orthostatic hypotension

In addition, severe hypertensive crisis may occur when MAO inhibitors are combined with food of high tyramine content—aged cheese, chicken livers, pickled herring, Chianti wine—or with many drugs, like sympathomimetic nose drops, antihistamines, antihypertensives, meperidine hydrochloride (Demerol), and caffeine. MAO inhibitors also interact with a wide variety of other medications.

As for contraindications, you should avoid using tricyclics with anticholinergic properties in patients with cardiovascular disease. Other contraindications for antidepressants are prostatic hypertrophy, thyrotoxicosis, renal diseases, and narrow-angle glaucoma.

Besides the foregoing precautions, other special considerations should be kept in mind. First, avoid barbiturates in depressed patients. They introduce the serious danger of suicide by overdosage, and they inhibit the actions of tricyclics by activating hepatic enzymes. This negative interaction produces lower plasma levels of tricyclics and requires higher doses of these antidepressants to obtain the same clinical effect.

Stimulants—amphetamines, phenmetrazine hydrochloride (Preludin), vitamins, and tonics—are not appropriate treatment for depression. They may give a patient a false sense of energy and alertness even though he is operating at diminished efficiency, and they may energize a suicide attempt. Stimulants may also produce a rebound letdown when discontinued, thus exacerbating depression.

While the use of any antidepressant drugs should be avoided in pregnancy, tricyclics may be given with no expectation of fetal harm if they are deemed essential to a pregnant woman's mental health.

Electroconvulsive therapy

Electroconvulsive therapy (ECT) should be considered for severely retarded or severely agitated patients, for patients whose conditions contraindicate antidepressants, and for some acutely suicidal patients. It can lead to rapid and dramatic remission of symptoms.

In standard ECT, a carefully controlled pulse of electrical energy is delivered to the patient's brain through a set of electrodes that is placed on his forehead. A tonic contraction is followed by a generalized clonic convulsion. (The actual muscular effects are modified by giving a short-acting muscle relaxant to those patients who have been anesthetized with a rapid-acting barbiturate.)

The usual course of treatment is six to 10 shocks over a three-week period. The specific mechanism of ECT is unknown. Some clinicians believe the electrical charge alters brain chemistry.

Electroshock therapy has the advantage of not producing the hypotension, drowsiness, and tremors sometimes seen with antidepressants. It does not present the risk of hypertensive crisis that may occur with MAO inhibitors. However, ECT may temporarily impair a patient's memory and cause him to be confused. And this technique does not prevent the recurrence of episodes.

Psychotherapy

The psychotherapeutic approach to depression has been used with apparent success in many instances. But there have been no sophisticated studies revealing which depressive symptoms it relieves—and to what degree or how rapidly. Moreover, no published studies show that psychotherapy causes more rapid or complete recovery than would take place in the natural course of acute depression. Nonetheless, numerous clinicians believe that psychotherapy is especially useful in patients suffering reactive depressions (psychotic or neurotic depressions triggered by specific stresses) or depressions accompanying developmental crises of life, such as menopause.

There are three principal types of psychotherapy directed against depression:

1. Short-term or time-limited psychotherapy, which is particularly effective for acute depression and unresolved grief. Such treatment focuses on clear precipitants, deals with losses and what they represent, and limits the degree of therapeutic involvement.

63

2. Family and group therapy, which can be of considerable value in the long run. They center on the interpersonal and familial relationships that are usually disrupted during depressive episodes. But their value in reducing symptoms in the acute stage is questionable.

3. A combination of psychotherapy and pharmacotherapy, which represents the best treatment in the acute phase. Drugs reduce symptom intensity and allow patients to utilize psychotherapy more effectively, which in turn may benefit long-term adjustment.

Table 4-1

Dosages for commonly used antidepressants

Antidepressant	Daily starting dose (mg)	Daily dosage range (mg)
Tricyclics		
Amitriptyline HCl (Elavil)	100	75-200
Desipramine HCl (Norpramin, Pertofrane)	75	75-300
Doxepin HCl (Adapin, Sinequan)	100	75-400
Imipramine HCl (Imavate, Janimine, Presamine, SK-Pramine, Tofranil)	100	75-300
Imipramine pamoate (Tofranil-PM)	100	75-300
Nortriptyline HCl (Elavil)	100	75-100
Protriptyline HCl (Vivactil)	30	10-40
MAO inhibitors		
Isocarboxazid (Marplan)	30	3-60
Phenelzine sulfate (Nardil)	30	10-90
Tranylcypromine (Parnate)	20	10-50
Miscellaneous agents		
Diazepam (Valium)	15	6-40
Perphenazine/amitriptyline HCl mixture (Etrafon, Triavil)	6/75	6/75-24/150
Thioridazine (Mellaril)	100	100-800

Suggested reading

Ayd, F.J., Jr. *Recognizing the Depressed Patient.* Grune and Stratton, 1961.

Enelow, A. *Depression in Medical Practice.* Marck & Co., 1970.

Gallant, Donald M., and Simpson, George M., eds. *Behavioral, Biochemical, Diagnostic and Treatment Concepts.* New York: Spectrum Publications, Inc., 1976.

Greenacre, Phyllis. *Affective Disorders.* Int. Univ. Press, 1953.

Kiev, Ari. "Somatic Manifestations of Depressive Disorders." Excerpta Medica, 1974.

5 Diagnosis and treatment of manic states

5 Diagnosis and treatment of manic states

The manic state, seen in manic-depressive illness, consists exclusively of manic episodes, or of at least one attack combining a depressive episode and a manic episode (circular type). This illness is usually recurrent and tends to be familial. An untreated manic state may continue for several months before remitting.

Manic episodes have these characteristics:

- Agitated gestures, talkativeness
- Increased energy and lack of need to sleep
- Reckless activity (spending sprees, foolish business investments)
- Distractibility
- Flight of ideas
- Exaggerated emotions, often with elation or euphoria
- Inflated self-esteem

The manic state must be differentiated from schizophrenia of the schizoaffective type (see chapters on schizophrenia). You should consider the characteristics of schizophrenics from F.J. Fish's discussion of Schneider's first-rank criteria. According to Fish, a schizophrenic:

Believes that he hears his voice or his thoughts spoken aloud

Hallucinates conversations in which he hears voices speaking about him in the third person, or hallucinates voices giving a running commentary

Has bodily hallucinations through which he feels sensations that he knows are produced outside his body

Believes that thoughts are withdrawn from his consciousness and thoughts inserted into it

Believes that he broadcasts his thoughts

Experiences delusions

Feels that all events—of feeling, drive, and volition—are arranged or influenced by others

The presence of any one of these criteria indicates schizophrenia and therefore differentiates schizophrenics from manic-depressives. Remember that a very accelerated manic, responding to every stimulus in his environment, may appear flagrantly psychotic, but yet is not schizophrenic. However, both manics and schizophrenics may suffer from paranoid ideation. Schizophrenics usually demonstrate blunted or inappropriate affect.

Diagnosis is easier in manics with pronounced symptoms than in those with milder forms. The initiative and energy of hypomanics may impel them to high administrative positions. If they do not overstep the bounds of reality, they strike awe in more phlegmatic workers and seem to be much better tolerated than patients with a corresponding level of depression. These milder forms are difficult to diagnose and may not require treatment.

Therapy for mania

Electroshock is only of historic importance in treating

mania. The introduction of electroconvulsive therapy (ECT) in the emergency rooms of psychiatric hospitals was seen as an advance in the treatment of severely manic patients, who often received two or three treatments a day for several days to calm them. This treatment of mania is still useful as backup in an emergency, but it is rarely instituted as preferred treatment.

Antipsychotic medication, however, has made control of the acute manic phase possible. Even today, this is the approach of choice for initiating treatment of an acute manic attack. Drugs in use include reserpine (Lemiserp, Rau-Sed, Resercen), chlorpromazine (Thorazine), and haloperidol (Haldol), with haloperidol the most favored. The major advantage of this drug is that while it reliably calms a manic patient, neither oral nor injectable form generally causes hypotension, and motor overactivity is reduced without overwhelming sedation. When first introduced, haloperidol was used in doses too low to control acute mania, but recent revisions in prescribing recommendations allow its use in doses up to 100 mg daily. Haloperidol, given repeatedly at adequate doses by the IM route, brings an extremely rapid response in a manic patient, so that he can be well managed within 48 hours.

Lithium carbonate

Cade, in Australia, was studying toxic constituents in the urine of manic patients in 1949. He accidentally observed that lithium carbonate promoted lethargy and had a calming action on manic patients. Previously it had been used to treat gout in the nineteenth century. The bromide of lithium was used to sedate patients at the turn of the century, but it fell into disuse along with other bromide compounds. Lithium chloride was introduced as a salt

71

substitute in 1949 but was quickly abandoned when it caused lithium intoxication.

In treatment, manics tolerate three to four times the dose of lithium carbonate that normal subjects can, until their mania breaks. Then they, too, may show toxic reactions to the lithium unless the dosage is reduced. One advantage of lithium is that there appears to be a correlation between serum level of the lithium ion and therapeutic and toxic results. A therapeutic level of 0.8-1.2 mEq/ liter and a maintenance level of 0.6-1.0 mEq/liter are desirable. The toxic level of lithium is 2.0 mEq/liter.

Lithium serum levels should be measured eight to 12 hours after the last dose is taken, because this is the method used in establishing norms. (Recently lithium levels have been monitored by testing saliva.)

Lithium carbonate, when used alone, requires five to 10 days to become effective. Because of this delay and because the toxicity level is quite close to the therapeutic level, a combination of lithium carbonate and an antipsychotic drug is generally accepted as the best treatment for an acute manic attack.

For an acute attack, you should divide the lithium dosage: 300 mg t.i.d. on the first day, followed by 600 mg t.i.d. on the second. Thereafter, adjust dosage between 1,500 mg and 2,500 mg daily according to the patient's lithium serum level. Check the level every other day. To maintain that level once an acute episode is under control, administer 300 to 1,500 mg daily, in a single dose if you wish, and test for lithium level once a month.

Precautions

Contraindications include serious cardiovascular disease, renal disease or a history of it in the family, analgesic abuse, kidney stones, diabetes mellitus, diastolic hypertension, and inadequate sodium intake. Patients should not take diuretics while on lithium-carbonate therapy, and they should supplement their sodium-chloride intake if active in hot weather. Extra salt prevents lithium toxicity secondary to hyponatremia induced by profuse sweating and also prevents nausea in certain patients taking single doses.

Before giving lithium carbonate, order these tests: electrolytes, CBC, white-cell differential count, creatinine, BUN, and 24-hour urine for volume, creatinine clearance, and protein excretion; also, do an ECG and check thyroid size and function. Side effects are gastrointestinal disturbances (nausea, vomiting, diarrhea, abdominal pain), muscle weakness, fine tremors, stiffness, dizziness, fullness of the head, blurred vision, thirst, and polyuria. Side effects not related to dosage include diffuse thyroid enlargement in six months to two years, nontoxic goiter, nephrogenic diabetes insipidus, and leukocytosis. Since renal damage has been reported, during therapy, the serum lithium should be monitored every week for the first month, every month for the first year, and every three months thereafter. Every six months, order BUN and urinalysis, and every year a 24-hour urine for volume, creatinine clearance, and protein excretion.

The marks of lithium toxicity are drowsiness, muscle twitching, coarse tremors and slurred speech followed by coma, increased muscle tone, convulsions, and even death as lithium serum levels increase. Levels above 2.0 mEq/liter are considered in the toxic range.

Lithium carbonate is of major benefit in preventing recurrent attacks of mania and, though useful in preventing recurrent episodes of depression, should be prescribed for this latter indication only if the patient has not

73

been responsive to long-term therapy with a tricyclic or MAO inhibitor. Most failures of lithium-carbonate pro-phylaxis occur during the first year. If a patient can re-main on a maintenance schedule without episodes for a year, it is very likely that the drug will be prophylactical-ly successful for him.

However, lithium carbonate is poor treatment for schizophrenia. In one study it aggravated the symptoms of patients with schizoaffective schizophrenia. Indeed, this characteristic may be useful in differential diagnosis.

The authors have administered a combination of halo-peridol and lithium carbonate to hundreds of patients with no observations of substantial irreversible brain damage. Yet four cases of brain damage have been reported with this therapy. These results warrant further investigation because the exact cause is not clear in these cases.

Suggested reading

Fish, F.J. *Schizophrenia*. Bristol, England: John Wright & Sons, p. 81, 1962.

Gershon, S., and Shopsin, B. *Lithium: Its Role in Psychiatric Research and Treatment*. Plenum Press, 1973.

"Lithium in the Treatment of Mood Disorders," N.I.M.H., National Clearinghouse for Mental Health Information Publ. #5033, 1970.

Lynn, E.J.; Satloff, A.; and Tinling, D.C. "Mania and Use of Lithium: A Three Year Study." *Am J Psychiat* 127(9): 1176-1180, 1971.

Neu, C.; DiMascio, A.; and Williams, D. "Saliva Lithium Levels: Clinical Applications." *Amer J Psychiat* 132(1): 66-68, 1975.

Prien, R.F.; Caffey, E.M.; and Klett, C.J. "Factors Associated With Treatment Success in Lithium Carbonate Prophylaxis." *Arch Gen Psychiat* 31: 189-192, 1974.

6 Diagnosis and treatment of anxiety states

Anxiety is a state of discomfort produced in a person by a generalized expectation of danger from an unknown source. This subjective state is analogous to fear, but it is different because the source of danger that produces fear is known. Qualitatively, three expressive components appear to make up the anxiety state and are experienced in varying degrees: apprehension, tension, and panic. Anxiety may be phasic or episodic and may have multiple remissions and exacerbations, or it may be chronic. It is frequently associated with somatic or visceral symptoms—cardiovascular, skeletal, and gastrointestinal. In uncomplicated cases, the prognosis is good.

More than 20 percent of all adult Americans experience episodes of anxiety that are long enough, severe enough, or disabling enough to require therapeutic intervention. Various theories have been proposed to explain the mechanisms of pathological anxiety states. The most prominent are these:

1. The Freudian psychoanalytic concept. Anxiety is a consequence of conflict between an individual's instinctual erotic or aggressive drives and the introjected values and morals of society (superego).

2. The Pavlovian theory. Here anxiety is a conditioned form of fear. The theory exists in two versions:

A. Unknown stimuli (internal or external) are unconsciously experienced as a threat. In turn, the threat provokes a series of somatic and visceral responses (fight or flight). It is identified as Cannon's theory.

77

B. Unknown stimuli (internal or external) evoke somatic or visceral responses. In turn, the responses cause the individual to subjectively sense and react to them. This is called the James Lange theory.

Manifestations of anxiety

Anxiety can affect every bodily system, alter every aspect of behavior, and color almost every mood state or emotion. These are its chief characteristics:

Behavioral signs or changes

Distractibility
Heightened reactivity
Lack of motivation
Increased speech disruptions
Increased rigidity of opinions
and behavior

Compulsiveness
Obsessive preoccupation
Repetitive motor acts
Decreased learning or
problem-solving ability

Emotional or mood-state changes

Increased apprehension
Excessive worry
Decreased frustration tolerance

Increased irritability
Sensitivity to shame and guilt
Emotional lability

Physiological responses or signs

Palpitations
Hyperventilation
Headaches
Dizziness
Urinary frequency
Excessive perspiration

Increased gastric secretions
Dermatological eruptions
(antigen-antibody reaction
disturbances)
Vague aches and pains
Motor restlessness
Altered sensory perception

Psychosomatic disorders often result from the foregoing bodily disruptions

Asthma	Hypertension
Cardiac neurosis	Insomnia
Peptic ulcer	Obesity
Eczema	Fatigue states
	General hypochondriasis

Management of anxious patients

Psychological or behavioral treatment involves modification of emotional states or behavioral ramifications by verbal means or by environmental manipulations. Verbal therapies attempt to uncover and to develop an understanding of causative mechanisms and thus bring about changes in the individual. Behavior therapies utilize learning theory principles (e.g., reinforcement, conditioning, extinction) to intervene more directly to develop effective methods of coping.

Individual psychoanalysis. For episodic anxiety states or transient situational anxiety reactions, psychoanalysis may be helpful—but it may be unnecessary at the same time. For chronic anxiety states, it uncovers conflicts and structures new adaptive and coping mechanisms.

Individual psychotherapy. In acute anxiety states supportive or reassurance therapy is useful, especially when directed to easing interpersonal conflicts and promoting emotional stability. For chronic anxiety, insight psychotherapy helps to resolve unconscious conflicts.

Group therapy. This form of treatment provides a supportive structure and forces interpersonal interactions. By itself, group therapy may be of limited use in reducing symptomatology in an acute anxiety state.

Behavior therapy. Various forms exist and are differ-

79

entially applied to different states. If stress stimuli evoking the anxiety are identifiable, as in specific phobic states, deconditioning procedures are extremely effective. Relaxation therapy is particularly beneficial for patients exhibiting autonomic or neuromuscular signs.

Environmental manipulation. Suggesting environmental changes—such as switching jobs—may reduce stress stimuli and may alleviate anxiety symptoms.

Pharmacological treatment. A wide variety of drugs are marketed for anxiety. They also have the capacity to produce, in varying degrees, sedation-hypnosis and muscle relaxation, but at the same time may interfere with motor and intellectual performance, and can cause tolerance, dependence, or addiction.

Barbiturates

Representatives of the barbiturate family are sodium butabarbital (Butisol Sodium), amobarbital (Amytal), and phenobarbital (Luminal, Eskabarb). At doses large enough to reduce anxiety, barbiturates are likely to impair motor or intellectual performance in comparison to the benzodiazepine derivatives mentioned further on. You should refrain from coadministering barbiturates and other psychotropic drugs such as chlorpromazine, imipramine, meprobamate, and MAO inhibitors. Barbiturates interact with them, causing the metabolism of both the barbiturates and all the other psychotropic drugs to be changed with consequences as yet not fully known. The authors, therefore, believe that barbiturates should be sparingly used for the treatment of anxiety states.

All three of these barbiturates, while relatively slow to take effect, are long-acting and efficacious as sedative-hypnotics. However, butabarbital and amobarbital are metabolized in the liver, like most barbiturates, and thus should not be given to patients with liver damage. Of all the drugs in this class, phenobarbital is renally excreted to the greatest extent in its unmetabolized form, so it may be preferable for patients with hepatic damage. But it probably should not be prescribed for patients with renal impairment.

Barbiturates quickly cause an increase in production of mitochondrial enzymes that speed up the metabolizing of many drugs—including the barbiturates themselves. Thus they induce metabolic tolerance, leading to increased dosage. The slower- and longer-acting barbiturates are more effective as sleep sustainers than sleep inducers. Somnolence is better accomplished by the faster- and shorter-acting barbiturate drugs.

In general, barbiturates should not be given to:

- Elderly and arteriosclerotic patients, because the drugs may produce a prolonged confusional state or exert a paradoxical effect.

- Seriously depressed patients, because the agents may aggravate their depression.

- Character-disorder patients who are disposed to drug dependency.

- Pregnant women—unless you exercise great caution—because barbiturates cross the placental barrier and may have a depressant effect on fetuses.

- Nursing mothers, because the drugs can be found in their milk.

Diphenylmethane derivatives

The most important property of these drugs—hydroxyzine (Atarax, Vistaril) and diphenhydramine (Benadryl)—is thought to be their antihistaminic activity. Nonetheless, they have many other valuable pharmacological actions, for example, anticholinergic action. Though thought to be useful in reducing anxiety, they are not as efficacious as the benzodiazepines. Furthermore, they have not been as readily accepted or used extensively as anxiolytic agents because they may increase muscle tone, lower convulsion threshold, and affect the peripheral autonomic system. On the other hand, diphenylmethane derivatives have no potential for habituation or physical dependence.

Hydroxyzine has been found to be of value in treating alcoholism, geriatric ailments, dermatological disorders, and preoperative anxiety. Diphenhydramine is useful in treating behavior disorders in children, drug-induced extrapyramidal side effects, dermatological disorders, and insomnia in geriatric patients.

Glycerol or propanediol derivatives

The drugs in this group originate in mephenesin, a potent muscle relaxant, and they possess this property in considerable degree. They also have sedative and anticonvulsant activity.

While numerous clinicians have reported the value of glycerol or propanediol derivatives in reducing anxiety, others still question their effectiveness, proclaiming them less effective than the benzodiazepines. Meprobamate (Miltown, Equanil) is said to induce liver microsomal enzymes and thus speed up its own metabolic inactivation. That action may lead to development of tolerance and dependence. In addition, meprobamate may produce addiction, with a typical withdrawal syndrome on abrupt discontinuation. Tybamate (Tybatran), however, has not been reported as producing addiction.

This group of drugs, the "central relaxants," are free of antihistaminic and anticholinergic activity. They accelerate breakdown of acetylcholine at synaptic junctions and thus depress multineuronal reflexes. Glycerol and propanediol derivatives may produce a multitude of dermatologic or allergic reactions: urticaria, angioneurotic edema, maculopapular rash, bullous dermatitis, nonthrombocytopenic purpura, and ecchymoses. And tybamate shows erratic absorption and a rapid plasma disappearance rate, which may lead to inconsistent clinical results.

β-Adrenergic blockers

The patient who develops symptoms of sympathetic discharge, such as sinus tachycardia or tremor, from a traumatic event may become conditioned to respond to stimuli in the same way. Such a patient then develops periodic anxiety and tachycardia, through a series of feedback mechanisms—a "signal-anxiety" syndrome—that are as yet incompletely understood. Such symptoms may be treated with β-adrenergic blockers, such as propranolol hydrochloride (Inderal, Inderide). There is marked variance in the blood levels of propranolol in different individuals with a given dose. Evidence of mild β-blockade is generally taken as a sign of adequate dosage. Propranolol's adverse effects include slowing of the pulse, negative inotropic cardiac effects, the occasional precipitation of asthma in susceptible individuals, feelings of coldness, and, occasionally, vivid and colorful nightmares. The abuse potential seems very low.

Antidepressants

The tricyclic antidepressants are useful in treating anxiety commonly found in tricyclic-responsive depression. They are also useful in treating panic attacks and agoraphobia. Patients whose anxiety comes in terrifying bursts of panic and those with severe anxiety associated with incapacitating agoraphobia both have panic anxiety and anticipatory anxiety. The panic may be relieved by judicious use of the tricyclics; among them, imipramine hydrochloride has had the most research done on it. The anticipatory anxiety is usually best managed by either supportive psychotherapy or behavior modification.

Benzodiazepine derivatives

Two of the most widely prescribed drugs in the United States are found in this class of anxiolytic drugs—diazepam (Valium) and chlordiazepoxide hydrochloride (Librium). These drugs are said to work by influencing the limbic system of the brain rather than the reticular activating system, thus altering affective states without reducing patient alertness. They relax skeletal muscles and act as anticonvulsants. They are also said to possess taming activity in animals; that is, they reduce aggressive behavior at doses that do not simultaneously cause sedation and inhibit motor responses.

As a group, the benzodiazepines are clearly superior in anxiolytic activity to the classes of antianxiety agents previously mentioned. They are also much less toxic at clinically useful doses. By contrast, the antipsychotic drugs, the so-called major tranquilizers, which are sometimes used as antianxiety agents in low doses, pose considerably more hazards and lack specificity and efficacy in reducing anxiety. The authors do not recommend routine use of the so-called major tranquilizers in the treatment of anxiety without psychoses.

As for the benzodiazepines marketed for anxiety reduction, there appear to be few differences in efficacy among them. Chlordiazepoxide, diazepam, clorazepate dipotassium (Tranxene), and prazepam (Verstran) have long biological half-lives and can accumulate in body tissues with repeated doses. They need to be given only once or twice a day, usually h.s. The drug with the longest half-life is prazepam, and during multiple-dose therapy with it, there is extensive accumulation of its metabolite desmethyldiazepam, which makes it possible to use prazepam as a once-daily anxiolytic. Chlorazepate requires acid hydrolysis in the stomach in order to achieve its psychoactive state. When given with antacids or in achlorhydric states, it may not achieve effective blood levels. Oxazepam (Serax), which does not accumulate in tissues, and lorazepam (Ativan), which only minimally accumulates in tissues, both have relatively short half-lives and must be given three or four times a day to be effective. Intramuscular chlordiazepoxide and diazepam are slowly and erratically absorbed and so should not be used when rapid sedative effects are desired. This is not true of lorazepam. Absorption of lorazepam from a deltoid intramuscular injection site is rapid and very nearly complete, giving it a distinct advantage over the others in this application. However, it is not an ideal intramuscular anxiolytic, since injection-site pain may be similar to that associated with chlordiazepoxide and diazepam.

The benzodiazepines, in contrast to most sedative-hypnotics, do not usually produce cardiovascular and respiratory depression when given orally or intramuscularly. Nor do they intensify clinically significant micro-

85

somal enzyme production, as do the barbiturates and meprobamate. As a result, their interactions with other drugs, such as sodium warfarin (Coumadin) and imipramine (Tofranil), do not constitute so great a problem.

Diazepam and lorazepam are frequently used as adjuncts in treating epileptic patients and when given intravenously are said to be of great value in rapidly relieving status epilepticus. But diazepam administered by the intravenous route may be painful. To reduce pain, it is suggested that venous blood be drawn into the syringe and mixed with the medication before injecting. Intravenous lorazepam produces sedative, anticonvulsant, and anterograde amnesic effects similar to those of diazepam but of longer duration, while sharing its cardiovascular safety. Profound anterograde amnesia lasting up to several hours has been reported after intravenous injection of large doses (4 mg) of lorazepam, which may be of particular benefit in anesthetic practice.

The benzodiazepines, particularly diazepam and chlordiazepoxide, have been shown to be of value in treating alcoholism, by controlling delirium tremens in the alcohol-withdrawal syndrome. Chlordiazepoxide and diazepam also increase aggressive-assertive behavior and even produce paradoxical rage reactions. (This effect does not occur with oxazepam or lorazepam). A physician prescribing these drugs should recognize that this phenomenon may result from drug administration rather than from mere exacerbation of underlying symptomatology. Though not classic antidepressants, the benzodiazepines elevate the depressed mood that occurs secondary to anxiety and relieve some symptoms, such as initial insomnia, of reactive depressions.

Absorption of benzodiazepines by geriatric patients is considerably slower than in younger adults, resulting in

86

the delay of beneficial clinical effects. And these medications, particularly diazepam and chlordiazepoxide, have potential for abuse when given in large doses for long periods. If discontinued abruptly they can cause classic withdrawal symptoms.

Teratogenicity have been attributed to benzodiazepines in occasional case reports and in a recent epidemiologic study. But the extremely wide use of these drugs with pregnant women throughout their pregnancies and over many years argues against this finding. Of course, the conservative approach is to refrain from giving these medications to pregnant patients unless it is essential to their well-being.

Ataxia, disinhibition, somnolence, headache, and dizziness are the most common adverse effects reported. There have been no reports of suicide by ingestion of benzodiazepines alone.

Pharmacotherapeutic precautions

It is important to remember that antianxiety drug dosage must be individualized and titrated to provide maximum relief with minimal adverse effects. Furthermore, anxiety is often phasic or episodic and may rapidly remit or diminish to a nonclinical level spontaneously or as a consequence of changes in environmental stress. Accordingly, treatment with antianxiety medications should be limited to short courses. Such therapy reduces the possibility of developing patient tolerance, with a concomitant loss of efficacy. And it reduces the need to increase dosages and thus avoids the risk of developing dependency or addiction. If the patient knows that relief for his anxiety is available, he may be willing to undergo stress without recourse to medication.

Some patients chronically complain of high levels of anxiety, so they may need to be maintained indefinitely on antianxiety drugs. In such cases, dosages should be kept relatively low, with periodic discontinuation of medication. These patients should be encouraged to use the drugs only when they really need medication. Just having the medication in a pocket or pocketbook, knowing it is always available, may give them enough security to do well without using it.

Table 6-1

Common subjective descriptions of anxiety experiences

Emotional	**Behavioral**
Anxious	Keyed up
Apprehensive	Panicky
Fearful	Phobic
Feeling of dread	Frightened for no reason
Nervous	Threatened
Overconcerned	
Worried	

Physical

Breathless	Restless
Choking sensations	Shaky
Dizzy	Sweating
Flushed	Tense
Giddy	Tightness in chest
Head pounding	Tire easily
Heart pounding	Trembling
Muscles tense	Urge to urinate

Table 6-2

Dosages for antianxiety agents

Antianxiety agent	Daily dosage range (mg)
Barbiturates	
Phenobarbital (Luminal, Eskabarb)	60-120
Sodium butabarbital (Butisol Sodium)	60-120
Amobarbital (Amytal)	60-120
Diphenylmethane derivatives	
Diphenhydramine (Benadryl)	50-200
Hydroxyzine (Atarax, Vistaril)	100-400
Glycerol or propanediol derivatives	
Meprobamate (Miltown, Equanil)	1,200-2,400
Tybamate (Tybatran)	1,050-2,500
Phenaglycodol (Ultran)	800-1,200
Benzodiazepine derivatives	
Chlordiazepoxide hydrochloride (Librium)	20-100
Diazepam (Valium)	10-60
Oxazepam (Serax)	30-120
Clorazepate dipotassium (Tranxene)	15-60
Prazepam (Verstran)	20-60
Lorazepam (Ativan)	2-6

Suggested reading

Greenblatt, D.J., and Shader, R.I. *Benzodiazepines in Clinical Practice*. Raven Press, 1974.

Hardin Branch, C. *Aspects of Anxiety*. Lippincott, 1965.

Mann, James. *Time-Limited Psychotherapy*. Harvard, 1973.

7 Psychotropic drugs in pregnancy:
Effects on the embryo, fetus, and neonate

7 Psychotropic drugs in pregnancy: Effects on the embryo, fetus, and neonate

American physicians prescribe at least one medication for more than 90 percent of their pregnant patients, and three or more drugs concomitantly for more than 20 percent.[1] All told, pregnant women take an average of 4.5 drugs (including iron, antiemetics, and diuretics) on their doctors' orders during the course of their pregnancies,[1] and heaven only knows how many more they take on their own. It's difficult to say precisely what percentage of these drugs are psychotropics, but a recent Australian review of prescriptions by general practitioners found that between 10 and 20 percent of women of childbearing age were taking an antidepressant.[2] Are these women—and their physicians—taking unnecessary risks with the lives of countless unborn children?

A wide variety of drugs taken by women of childbearing age and women who are pregnant has been documented to profoundly affect the unborn child, but as far as psychotropic drugs are concerned, fears of teratogenicity—fears based on data from animal studies, possible biochemical mechanisms, or reputed instances of drug-induced toxic effects—have not been borne out by the evidence. On the contrary, the medical literature shows that these drugs pose relatively little hazard for the fetus and the newborn. Permanent or long-lasting adverse effects occur no more frequently among births to women treated with psychotropics than they do among women treated with nonpsychotropic drugs or no drugs.

No cautious physician should or would prescribe a

psychotropic for a pregnant woman, especially in the first trimester, unless she urgently needed it. Undoubtedly, any drug taken by a patient at any stage of pregnancy, or by a woman who later becomes pregnant, can affect her unborn child, and few drugs are FDA-certified as safe for use in pregnancy. So caution is certainly called for, and it requires knowing which psychotropics are most likely to affect the fetus or infant and when and how they exert their effects.

Various mechanisms are operant at different stages of pregnancy to create hazards: chromosomal defects before conception, fetal damage, spontaneous abortions or premature births, labor and delivery problems, birth abnormalities, and excretion of drugs in mother's milk.

Chromosomal abnormalities

Drugs taken by a woman before she conceives or between conception and implantation may cause chromosomal abnormalities in the embryo. Duration of treatment, dosage level, and the number of drugs taken affect the frequency of such anomalies as chromosomal gaps or breaks and haploid cells. Such effects have been reported with perphenazine (Trilafon), chlorpromazine (Thorazine), and lithium carbonate (Eskalith, Lithane).

The relationship between chromosomal abnormalities and teratogenicity, however, is not clear-cut. Generally, if a teratogenic drug has its impact before implantation (the first week after conception), the embryo either resists those effects and develops normally or is grossly affected and soon aborts spontaneously.

Fetal damage

During most of pregnancy, the crucial question is whether a drug enters fetal blood. Most drugs are thought to cross the placental barrier by simple diffusion, in proportion to their lipid solubility, and detectable concentrations of all psychotropics have been reported in fetal circulation. In particular, phenothiazines have been noted in various concentrations in the fetal brain and liver.[3] Adverse effects may occur because specific mechanisms for drug detoxification or inactivation—oxidation, reduction, hydrolysis, or conjugation of the compound with substances such as glucuronic acid—are not sufficiently developed in the fetus. Chlorpromazine may interfere with bilirubin metabolism by binding serum albumin. Nevertheless, evidence of accentuated neonatal jaundice or liver toxicity due to chlorpromazine is not documented by the literature.

On the other hand, barbiturate levels in fetal blood may reach three-quarters of maternal blood levels. Thus barbiturates have a real potential for depressing fetal respiratory centers.

During the organ-forming period, the second through seventh weeks of gestation, the embryo is extremely sensitive to teratogenic drugs. Most congenital malformations, including drug-induced ones—especially of the skeletal system, eyes, ears, and heart—originate in this period. Drugs taken by the mother between 60 days and term (the fetal period) usually don't cause major deformities, as organ-system formation is complete.

Spontaneous abortions or premature births

Occasional reports have been published associating psychotropics with spontaneous abortions, premature births, or increased fetal morbidity. But the most extensive reviews of these phenomena—by Sobel,[4] Ayd,[5] Shader,[6] and Van Waes and Van de Velde[7]—report no statistically significant increase among patients given chlorpromazine, haloperidol (Haldol), or meprobamate (Equanil, Miltown) even during the first trimester, compared with nondrug-treated groups.

Birth abnormalities

Reports of teratogenic effects of phenothiazines, butyrophenones, and lithium in humans have been published. Here, too, closer scrutiny indicates that women taking chlorpromazine, thioridazine (Mellaril), trifluoperazine (Stelazine), perphenazine, or haloperidol had abnormal births of all types to no greater degree than controls not treated with drugs. For example, after an initial report of drug-induced abnormality, Moriarity and Nance surveyed 480 women given trifluoperazine during pregnancy.[8] They found abnormalities in 1.1 percent of these births, and in 1.6 percent of the control births.

Szabo[9] and other investigators[10] have found eye defects, cleft palate, and various other congenital malformations in the offspring of pregnant animals given lithium. But animal teratogenicity doesn't necessarily mean human teratogenicity, and reviews of cases in Scandinavia, Canada, and the United States have failed to record a greater incidence of congenital malformations among babies born to lithium-treated mothers than that expected in the general population.

Similarly, tricyclic antidepressants reportedly have been associated with a limited number of cases of limb-reduction deformities and other malformations. Yet data from the Finnish Register of Congenital Malformations, from the Australian Drug Evaluation Committee, and from the Australian Morbidity Survey—in which thousands of cases were studied—do not support the contention that tricyclics are a cause of such abnormalities.

More recently, an article in the *New England Journal of Medicine* speculated that meprobamate and chlordiazepoxide hydrochloride (Librium) might be teratogenic when taken during the first six weeks of gestation.[11] The specter of drug-induced anomalies was raised by the authors in spite of the fact that their own statistical analysis revealed no significant increase in congenital anomalies between the two groups of drug-treated patients and the no-drug comparison groups. Further, a review of records of 50,000 pregnancies in the Collaborative Perinatal Project failed to find any evidence of ill effects of either drug on the newborn.[12]

Labor and delivery problems

Drugs given during pregnancy, especially during the last trimester, may affect labor, delivery, and the infant's perinatal period. For example, when phenothiazines are given in the last trimester, they may cause extrapyramidal reactions such as posturing or tongue protrusion lasting many months, respiratory depression and hypoxia lasting up to one week, neonatal jaundice and hyperbilirubinemia, and melanin deposits in the eyes.[13]

However, when thioridazine, haloperidol, perphenazine, prochlorperazine (Compazine), or promazine hydrochloride (Sparine) is used during the last few days prior to delivery—as a labor adjunct, to reduce emotional tension, to control nausea and vomiting, or to potentiate analgesia—most reports claim no negative effects on the newborn.

Likewise, diazepam (Valium), in relatively low doses given before delivery—like the phenothiazines—does not affect duration of labor, increase the number of operative deliveries, or obviously affect the infant. But when given in doses greater than 100 mg, it has been reported, in a few cases, to depress respiration and reflexes and cause severe asphyxia with cyanosis in the newborn.[14] In addition, temporary hypoactivity, hypotonicity, and hypothermia have been observed by clinicians.

Lithium generally poses no extra risk in delivery. Cases have been reported, however, in which pregnant women taking lithium in usual doses, with serum lithium levels within the normal therapeutic range a few days prior to delivery, nevertheless showed effects of lithium toxicity during delivery. In these cases, the women had been on a low-salt weight-reducing diet and had been taking diuretics.

Although sodium depletion alone may cause lithium toxicity, in this case the problem was complicated by the changes in renal lithium clearance that occur during pregnancy and at delivery. Lithium clearance rises in pregnant women, causing serum levels to fall. A dosage increase may therefore be necessary to prevent the patient's relapse. But at delivery, renal clearance falls, and serum levels may rise rapidly to toxic levels. It's important to check serum levels often at this time, and to consider the possibility of temporarily discontinuing lithium administration until after delivery.

Lithium levels in the newborn. In the newborn, lithium has been reported to cause cyanosis, poor sucking, rapid respiration, tachycardia, and flaccid muscle tonus.

Excretion of drugs in mother's milk

Psychotropic drugs may appear in the breast milk of nursing mothers. Infants are vulnerable because they have not developed adequate metabolic or elimination mechanisms to cope with such medications.

Nursing mothers excrete the psychotropics in varying amounts:

- Drugs not transmitted in mother's milk:

    Amitriptyline (Elavil) and its metabolites, nortriptyline (Aventyl) and its metabolites, desipramine, and, perhaps, imipramine

- Drugs transmitted in trace or negligible amounts (having no effects on infants):

    Chlorpromazine, thioridazine, mesoridazine (Serentil), prochlorperazine, trifluoperazine, and tranylcypromine (Parnate)

- Drugs transmitted in modest amounts (possibly affecting infants):

    Haloperidol, chlordiazepoxide, oxazepam (Serax), clorazepate dipotassium (Tranxene), and diazepam (which has caused EEG changes, lethargy, and weight loss in infants—and possibly long-lasting neonatal jaundice or kernicterus—because it is metabolized by conjugation with glucuronic acid)

- Drugs transmitted in appreciable amounts (calling for toxicity monitoring of a nursing mother who takes them):

    Meprobamate (for which no documentation of toxicity exists), lithium compounds (the carbonate form of which appears in breast milk at half the mother's serum lithium level and in the infant's serum at one-third to one-half the mother's level); most authorities agree that mothers on lithium should not breast feed,

101

though documentation of toxicity in infants is not available.

Conclusion

Evidence presented in this chapter demonstrates that psychotropic drugs may be administered to pregnant women without unduly endangering fetuses or newborns.

When patients who are taking psychotropics are compared with patients who are not, there is no significant difference in occurrence of long-lasting or permanent adverse effects.

Fears of harm have originated in data from animal studies, knowledge of possible biochemical mechanisms, and instances of alleged toxic effects induced by drugs. Teratogenicity of drugs in animals does not necessarily imply teratogenicity in humans. Moreover, large-scale controlled surveys of patients have not supported the worst fears of certain clinicians.

No careful practitioner would recommend that psychotropic medications be given to pregnant women, especially in their first trimester, unless the patient was in urgent need of them. However, any physician who must prescribe these agents to such women can do so knowing that their appropriate and judicious use has not been demonstrated to be detrimental to fetuses or neonates.

Two warnings on prescribing psychotropics

1. Do not prescribe diuretics or low-sodium diets for pregnant women, because either course reduces lithium excretion. The consequent rise in serum-lithium level may cause toxicity in mothers or neonates.

2. Take a complete drug history before prescribing psy-

chotropics that may interact with other drugs to seriously damage the fetus. Remember that a pregnant woman often ingests a number of over-the-counter drugs as well as those you prescribe for her.

References

1. Catz, C.S., and Abuelo, D. "Drugs and Pregnancy." *Drug Therapy* 4:79, 1974.

2. Rowe, I.L. "Prescriptions of Psychotropic Drugs by General Practitioners: II Antidepressants." *Med J Aust* 1:642, 1973.

3. Adamsons, K., and Joelsson, I. "The Effects of Pharmacologic Agents Upon the Fetus and Newborn." *Am J Obstet Gynecol* 96:437, 1966.

4. Sobel, E.E. "Fetal Damage Due to ECT, Insulin Coma, Chlorpromazine or Reserpine." *Arch Gen Psychiat* 2:606, 1960.

5. Ayd, F. "Meprobamate Drug Pregnancy." *International Drug Therapy Newsletter* 6:16, 1971.

6. Shader, R.I. "Pregnancy and Psychotropic Drugs," in Shader, R.I., and DiMascio, A., eds. *Psychotropic Drug Side Effects.* Baltimore: Williams and Wilkins, 1970, p. 206.

7. Van Waes, A., and Van deVelde, E. "Safety and Evaluation of Haloperidol in the Treatment of Hyperemesis Gravidarum." *J Clin Pharmacol* 9:224, 1969.

8. Moriarity, A.J., and Nance, N.R. "Trifluoperazine and Pregnancy." *Can Med Assoc J* 88:375, 1963.

9. Szabo, K.T. "Teratogenicity of Lithium in Mice." *Lancet* 2:849, 1969.

10. Schou, M., and Amdisen, A. "Lithium Teratogenicity." *Lancet* 1:1132, 1971.

11. Milkovich, L., and Van den Berg, B.J. "Effects of Prenatal Meprobamate and Chlordiazepoxide Hydrochloride on Human Embryonic and Fetal Development." *N Eng J Med* 291:1268, 1974.

12. Hartz, S.C.; Heinonen, O.P.; Shapiro, S.; et al. "Antenatal Exposure to Meprobamate and Chlordiazepoxide in Relation to Malformations, Mental Development and Childhood Mortality." *N Eng J Med* 292:726, 1975.

13. Levy, W., and Wisneski, K. "Chlorpromazine Causing Extrapyramidal Dysfunction in Newborn Infant of Psychotic Mother." *NY State J Med* 74:684, 1974.

14. McCarthy, G.T.; O'Connel, B.; and Robinson, A.E. "Blood Levels of Diazepam in Infants of Two Mothers Given Large Doses of Diazepam During Labor." *J Obstet Gynecol Br Commw* 80:349, 1973.

8 Psychotropic drugs in childhood disorders

Three major groups of psychiatric disorders in childhood are extensively treated with psychotropic drugs: psychotic disorders, psychoneurotic disorders, and minimal brain dysfunctions.

I **Psychotic disorders,** variously labeled childhood schizophrenia, early infantile autism, or childhood psychosis. They are characterized by early onset (within the first year) of symptoms that generally are resistant to all forms of treatment. Thus, prognosis is not too favorable. The symptomatology generally consists of one or more of the following:

— Relationship abnormalities, such as withdrawal, lack of pleasure in, or even recognition of interpersonal social interactions
— Speech development failure, with lack of comprehension or verbal communication
— Perceptual aberrations, with excessive, diminished, or unpredictable responses to stimuli; hallucinations
— Motor pattern abnormalities, such as constant rocking, hypo- and hyperactivity, aimless repetitive stereotyped movements, or bizarre posturing
— Reality relationship impairment, as demonstrated by lack of self-awareness, and self-mutilative behavior
— Unpredictable and/or extreme emotional reactions involving aggression, fear or anxiety, or apathy and flatness of expression

II **Psychoneurotic disorders,** which consist of various

107

relatively specific states affecting limited aspects of behavior. They usually occur after a few years of normal development, and are usually associated with some traumatic event. Prognosis is good. The different types of psychoneurotic disorders include:

— Anxiety states, often characterized by hypervigilance, fear, tenseness, exhibition of nervous energy (nail biting, tics), increased dependency on mother
— Phobic states, with fear of specifiable situations or stimuli coupled with avoidance behavior. Fear of animals and school phobias are two common ones.
— Depressive reactions, manifested by expressions of great sadness or loneliness, dysphoric moods, withdrawal, feelings of guilt or shame, low self-esteem, and insecurity. Said to occur seldom in the pre-adolescent. Difficult to diagnose.

III Minimal brain dysfunction, also called the hyperkinetic syndrome, hyperactivity, or learning disability. It is said to occur in 3 to 7 percent of the population under 14, and is noted most often in boys. (The ratio is three to one over girls.) It tends to reduce in intensity by puberty. But because of behavior patterns learned during formative years, maladaptive behavior problems and personality traits persist. Although sometimes noted earlier, it is usually not really recognized until the child starts school. Such children exhibit a cluster of symptoms that affect all spheres of functioning and that include:

— Hyperactivity with constant driven movements
— Short attention span; inability to concentrate for any length of time. This often appears as a learning deficit in a child capable of performing above average.

— Coordination abnormalities, or motor maturation lag (one of the "soft neurological" signs)
— Affective lability, with low frustration tolerance and aggressive behavior, temper tantrums, crying
— Impulsiveness, with acting-out and self-serving, disruptive behavior
— Impaired interpersonal relationships with peers and adults, as shown by a dominating attitude toward peers—resulting in relative friendlessness—and failure to respond to authority

Nonpharmacologic treatment

The treatment approach needs to involve corrective experiences for disrupted areas of functioning. Among the most frequently used procedures, often used in combination, are:

1. Individual psychotherapy. Development of a relationship is attempted through verbal or nonverbal (play therapy) means, designed to uncover unconscious conflicts underlying symptoms. Not very successful in psychotic disorders or minimal brain dysfunctions.

2. Operant conditioning techniques, which use positive or negative reinforcement to desensitize or extinguish specific behaviors, or to condition and establish desired patterns of response. Said to be quite useful in psychoneurotic disorders, but only of limited effectiveness in psychotic disorders and minimal brain dysfunctions.

3. Remedial or educational procedures, used to correct specific educational or learning deficits that may have been caused by, or may cause, psychological problems.

4. Residential or milieu therapy. The patient is placed in

109

a new environment where multiple treatment approaches can be applied in a situation removed from possible familial or environmental etiological stressors.

5. Family therapy: The parents, siblings, and child are brought together to explore areas of conflict or to develop supportive attitudes.

Pharmacological treatment

In the psychotic disorders, the major drugs are the same as those used in treating adults. But their effectiveness in eliminating core symptoms of childhood psychoses has yet to be firmly established. Furthermore, it is impossible to say that one drug is more effective than another for any psychotic symptomatology. Presently, *only the following* are FDA-approved for use in children:

Aliphatic phenothiazines

● Chlorpromazine (Thorazine, Chlor-PZ). Used in acutely agitated states, and said to reduce overactivity, impulsivity, acting-out, and aggressiveness.

Can often produce drowsiness, lethargy, fatigue, and apathy as well as mild disorganization, increased irritability, and vivid dreams. Hypotension has not been mentioned as a problem, and extrapyramidal symptoms (EPS) have rarely been reported. Abnormalities in hematological, renal, and liver-function tests have been documented in adults, but not in children. Similarly, the skin and eye pigmentation seen in adults on long-term treatment has not been documented in children.

In children with a history of epilepsy or organic brain damage, an increase in seizures has often been noted after chlorpromazine.

110

● Triflupromazine (Vesprin). Not as extensively examined, yet said to be as effective as chlorpromazine. Produces same side effects with the additional warning to observe closely for extrapyramidal symptoms.

Piperidine phenothiazines

● Thioridazine (Mellaril). While the symptoms of hyperactivity, aggressiveness, acting-out, and self-abusiveness are decreased, core schizophrenic symptoms are seldom documented as having improved. Aggressive, assaultive behavior is mentioned as being improved with thioridazine more often than any other symptom—and to a greater degree than with any other drug.

Thioridazine is remarkably free of side effects, with lethargy and drowsiness being the most common. Hematological, renal, and liver-function tests reported to be within normal ranges, and EPS extremely rare.

In contrast to chlorpromazine, thioridazine has been reported to reduce seizure frequency when given to children with epilepsy or organic brain damage.

Piperazine phenothiazines

● Trifluoperazine (Stelazine). Reported to reduce hyperactivity, impulsiveness, and aggressiveness. Activates hypoactive and withdrawn children. The claim is made—but questioned by some—that trifluoperazine is the drug of choice in autistic children.

The drug rarely produces drowsiness or motor inhibition, but is more likely to cause hyperactivity, restlessness, irritability, and increased apprehension or anxiety. No hematological, renal, or liver changes have been reported. While not given as often to seizure-prone children, trifluoperazine has not been associated with an increase in seizure frequency. The major side effect (principally within the first 10 days) is a high incidence of EPS—especially in boys. These reactions—oculogyric crises, head and neck dystonias, laryngeal spasms, and akathisia—are so dramatic that many physicians immediately stop treatment with the drug, even though the symptoms may be quickly managed by an antiparkinson agent or diphenhydramine (Benadryl).

● Prochlorperazine (Compazine). Has not achieved wide usage in children, either because it does not have comparable clinical effectiveness or, more likely, because of the relative frequency of dramatic and bizarre extrapyramidal symptoms. It should be used cautiously.

Thioxanthene derivatives

● Chlorprothixene (Taractan). The only drug of this class FDA-approved for children. The drug is claimed to be effective in relieving anxiety and decreasing hyperactivity and impulsivity in psychotic disorders. Adverse effects, as noted in the limited published studies, are few and mild. They consist of drowsiness, ataxia, and development of a "worse disposition." As with the phenothiazines, laboratory tests show no blood, kidney, or liver changes—other than an occasional slight and transient leukopenia.

In children receiving antipsychotic drugs over long periods, treatment withdrawal has been reported to produce a series of neurological or muscle movements that may persist for many months. These symptoms are considered by some to be the pediatric equivalent of tardive dyskinesia.

In childhood psychoneurotic disorders, some drugs used to treat anxiety and depression in adults have been

112

used and are FDA-approved for children. *Of the antianxiety drugs* available for adults, representatives from two chemical classes are often used in children:

Benzodiazepines

Chlordiazepoxide (Librium) and diazepam (Valium) are reported to be valuable for reducing anxiety in school-phobic children, and overactivity and impulsivity in neurotic, but not psychotic, children.

The main side effect noted is severe drowsiness—with associated muscle weakness and dizziness. Paradoxical rage reactions with children "going wild and losing control" have been reported, as well as increased anxiety and depression in some patients. Blood, kidney, and liver-function tests have not shown significant changes after either drug. No problems have been encountered in epileptic patients, and some clinicians use diazepam as an anticonvulsant adjunct.

Hypotension, nausea, and drowsiness have been reported in up to 25 percent of children taking diazepam. Increased hyperactivity, anxiety, and euphoria have also been reported.

Substituted propanediols

Meprobamate (Equanil, Miltown) and tybamate (Tybatran, Solacen). Meprobamate was evaluated in children shortly after its introduction into psychiatry, especially as a treatment for managing behavioral and physical problems associated with the convulsive disorders, rather than just for anxiety reduction. However, few studies have been carried out in the last 15 years. Studies with tybamate in children also have seldom been done, but the drugs are FDA-approved for use in children over six.

Their specific areas of functional value for children do not appear clearly documented.

Side effects of meprobamate in children are drowsiness, ataxia, dizziness, paradoxical excitement or hyperactivity, nausea, and allergic rashes. In addition, meprobamate has been reported to precipitate seizures in epileptic patients, and convulsions during withdrawal.

While the *antidepressants* are as old as the phenothiazines and are prescribed about as often in adult psychiatry, there is a dearth of studies assessing their effects in children—other than in the treatment of enuresis and behavior disorders where overactivity, impulsivity, and acting-out are present. Depression being a rare phenomenon in children, few studies have been done with antidepressants that show significant mood evaluation. Antidepressants have been reported to aggravate schizophrenic symptomatology.

Iminodibenzyl derivatives

Of the most widely used antidepressants, only imipramine (Tofranil, Presamine) is currently FDA-approved for use in children—and then only for the treatment of enuresis. Because it can be treated by an antidepressant, some clinicians have theorized that enuresis is therefore a depressive-equivalent symptom in children. In studies where imipramine has been given to nonenuretic children, it has been helpful in reducing overactivity and impulsivity. Accordingly, some have theorized that the hyperkinetic syndrome should be considered a "masked depression." Recent studies have reported imipramine to be effective also in the treatment of school phobias.

As with other drugs possessing anticholinergic properties, the main side effects are dry mouth, excessive

114

perspiration, drowsiness, and constipation. In addition, increased aggressiveness has been reported in children given imipramine.

In minimal brain dysfunction (or the hyperkinetic syndrome), drugs from a number of diverse groups with diverse clinical utility in adults have been tried (i.e., thioridazine or chlorpromazine—antipsychotics; imipramine—an antidepressant; chlordiazepoxide and diazepam—antianxiety agents; and amphetamines, methylphenidate, deanol, and pemoline—stimulating drugs).

While claims of effectiveness are made for all these types, stimulants are the most widely used FDA-approved drugs for this purpose. These drugs, which cause stimulation in adults, produce "paradoxical" quieting and slowing in children, as well as improvement of the other minimal brain dysfunction deficits.

As with all drugs used in childhood psychiatric disorders, drugs used in minimal brain dysfunction (MBD) symptomatology should be only a part of a total treatment program—although without them, the other components of the program may be rather ineffective.

The four major drugs for MBD are:

Amphetamines (Dexedrine or Benzedrine)

Amphetamines rapidly produce striking changes in the total behavior pattern—increasing attention span and social perceptiveness; decreasing hyperactivity, impulsiveness, and aggressiveness; and improving emotional stability. As a result, the child may show improved performance in school. The drugs are short-acting, and often require two doses per day. The improvements noted above quickly disappear if medication is terminated.

Commonly noted side effects include insomnia, headaches, increased disorganization, loss of appetite and weight, pallor and coldness of skin, and irritability. These occur early in treatment and are usually transient.

When these drugs are given continuously over long periods, they may cause weight and height growth inhibition. Cardiovascular effects, such as hypertension and tachycardia, have also been reported.

Addiction or habituation (as has been noted in adults and late adolescents) has not been reported in these young children.

Methylphenidate (Ritalin)

This drug produces the same improvement in behavior patterns as do the amphetamines.

The side effects are similar, although often not of as great intensity. Skin pallor is seldom noted and growth (height and weight) is not significantly reduced with long-term use, as is seen with amphetamines. While I.Q. level is not increased with either the amphetamines or methylphenidate, considerable improvement in scholastic performance may often be noted.

Deanol (Deaner)

Deanol, a postulated acetylcholine precursor, was used considerably in the 1960s. While early studies claimed the drug reduced overactivity and aggressiveness and improved attention and memory, later studies did not in general confirm these findings within the recommended dosage range.

Side effects were rarely reported, but some evidence indicates the drug is contraindicated in epilepsy.

Pemoline (Cylert)

This drug has also been reported to be a useful adjunct in

116

the treatment of MBD symptomatology. In contrast to the stimulants mentioned here, onset of action is gradual, and with the recommended schedule of dosage increase, significant clinical benefit may not be noted until after three to four weeks. It has a long biological half-life and can thus be readily given once a day (early in the morning). It is said to have few sympathomimetic effects and limited, if any, potential for abuse or addiction.

Side effects reported for pemoline include insomnia, transient anorexia, nausea, dizziness, and in rare instances, hallucinations.

Drug dosages in childhood disorders

The following outline gives the FDA-recommended *oral* dosages for children of specific ages.

While children have been found to be able to tolerate high doses of most of the drugs listed, prudent treatment consists of starting the medications at low levels and then individualizing dosage until a satisfactory response is obtained or the upper recommended level is reached. Once the behavior change is noted, the drug dosage should be dropped to the lowest possible level that maintains improvement. Periodic discontinuation is suggested to determine if the drug still is necessary.

Any physician choosing to treat a child with a greater than recommended dose would be wise to clearly write in the patient's records the need and rationale for doing so.

These drugs should be given only to children in whom the syndrome is relatively chronic, affects a number of areas of functioning, does not appear to be a reaction to environmental stresses, and who are enrolled in a total treatment program. The medications may make the children more amenable to other treatments, and should

117

not be thought of as curative in and of themselves.

I Antipsychotic agents

Phenothiazine derivatives

— Aliphatics

Chlorpromazine (Thorazine, Chlor-PZ). Dosage: Children under 5 (or 50 pounds), not over 40 mg/day. Children 5-12 (50-100 pounds), 3-6 mg/kg, but not over 250 mg/day, except in unmanageable cases.

Triflupromazine (Vesprin). Not for children under 2½. Dosage: 1 mg/lb, up to a maximum daily dose of 150 mg in divided doses.

— Piperidines

Thioridazine (Mellaril). Not for children under 2. Dosage: Ages 2-12, 0.5-3 mg/kg daily. Moderate disorders—10 mg b.i.d. or t.i.d. Severe disorders—25 mg b.i.d. or t.i.d., increased gradually until optimum effects are obtained.

— Piperazines

Trifluoperazine (Stelazine). For psychotic and mentally defective children. Dosage: Ages 6-12, 1 mg daily or b.i.d., up to 15 mg/day.

Prochlorperazine (Compazine). Not for children under 20 pounds or 2 years. Dosage in child psychiatry and behavior disorders: Ages 2-12, starting dosage is 2½ mg b.i.d. or t.i.d. *Do not give more than 10 mg the first day.* Ages 2-5, total daily dosage usually does not exceed 20 mg. Ages 6-12, total daily dosage usually does not exceed 25 mg.

118

Butyrophenones

— Haloperidol (Haldol). Dosage: 0.15-0.3 mg/kg. Children 5-12, 2-5 mg/day. Children over 12, 4-10 mg/day.

Thioxanthene derivatives

— Chlorprothixene (Taractan). Dosage: Children over 6, 10-25 mg t.i.d. or q.i.d.

— Thiothixene (Navane). Dosage: Children 6-12, 10-24 mg/day. Children over 12, 15-60 mg/day.

II Antidepressant agents

Tricyclics

— Iminodibenzyl derivatives

Imipramine (Tofranil, Presamine). Dosage in enuresis: 0.5-2.5 mg/kg. Children over 6, 25 mg/night; if no relief in one week, increase to 50 mg/night. Children over 12, up to 75 mg/night. Dosage in conduct and depressive disorders: Start at 1 mg/kg/day and increase to 2-5 mg/kg/day. Dosage in separation anxiety: 25-200 mg/day.

III Amphetamine and amphetaminelike stimulants

— Amphetamine sulfate (Benzedrine). Not for children under 3. Dosage: Ages 3-5, start with 5 mg/day. Daily dosage may be raised in increments of 5 mg/week until optimal response is obtained. Ages 6 and older, start with 10 mg daily or b.i.d. Daily dosage may be increased in increments of 10 mg/week until optimal response is obtained.

— Dextroamphetamine (Dexedrine). Not for children under 3. Dosage: Ages 3-5, 2.5 mg daily to start. Daily dosage may be increased in increments of 2.5 mg/week until optimal response is obtained. Ages 6 and older, start with 5 mg daily or b.i.d. Daily dosage may be increased in increments of 5 mg/week until optimal response is obtained. Maximum dose: 40 mg/day.

— Methylphenidate (Ritalin). Not for children under 6. Dosage: Ages 6-12, start with small doses (e.g., 5 mg before breakfast, 5 mg before lunch), with a gradual increase of 5-10 mg weekly. *A daily dose above 80 mg is not recommended.*

— Deanol (Deaner). Dosage: 300 mg in the morning. After three weeks, if satisfactory improvement has occurred, most children may be maintained on 100 mg daily.

— Pemoline (Cylert). Not for children under 6. Dosage: Ages 9 and older, start at 37.5 mg/day in a single dose; increase at weekly intervals by 18.75 mg until the desired clinical effect is obtained, up to a maximum daily dose of 112.5 mg.

IV Antianxiety agents

Benzodiazepines

— Chlordiazepoxide (Librium). Not for children under 6. Dosage: Ages 6-12, 5 mg b.i.d. to q.i.d. (May be increased in some children to 10 mg b.i.d. or t.i.d.)

— Diazepam (Valium). Not for children under 6 months. Dosage: Ages 6 months-12 yr, 1-2½ mg t.i.d. or q.i.d. initially; increase dosage gradually as needed and tolerated.

— Lorazepam (Ativan). Not for children under 12. Dosage: Children over 12, 2 mg/day.

Substituted propanediols (glycol or glycerol derivatives)

— Meprobamate (Equanil, Miltown). Not for children under 6. Dosage: Ages 6-12, 100-200 mg b.i.d. or t.i.d.

— Tybamate (Tybatran, Solacen). Not for children under 6. Dosage: Ages 6-12, 20-35 mg/kg daily in 3-4 equally divided doses.

V Antiparkinson drugs

— Diphenhydramine hydrochloride (Benadryl). Dosage in acute dystonic reaction: Under age 6, 12.5-25 mg IM. Ages 6-12, 25-50 mg IM. Dosage in other extrapyramidal reactions: Under age 6, 12.5-50 mg/day. Children over 6, 25-100 mg/day.

— Benztropine mesylate (Cogentin). Dosage: Under age 12, 0.5-1.0 mg/day. Children over 12, 0.5-5 mg/day.

— Trihexyphenidyl hydrochloride (Artane, Tremin). Dosage: Under age 12, 0.5-5 mg/day. Children over 12, 1-10 mg/day.

VI Anticonvulsants

— Phenytoin sodium (Dilantin) and barbiturates. Not indicated in nonepileptic children.

— Carbamazepine (Tegretol). May be helpful in motor overactivity or aggressive behavior. Dosage: Ages 6-

121

12, start with 200 mg/day, then increase. Children over 12, start with 200 mg b.i.d., then increase. Therapeutic serum level: 4-8 mcg/ml.

Suggested reading

Campbell, M., and Shapiro, T. "Therapy of Psychiatric Disorders of Childhood," in *Manual of Psychiatric Therapeutics*. R. Shader, ed. Little, Brown & Co., 1975, pp. 137-162.

Rapaport, J.L. "Pediatric Psychopharmacology in Depression," in *Progress in Psychiatric Drug Treatment*. D. Klein and R. Gittleman-Klein, eds. Brunner-Mazel, 1976.

Engelhardt, D.M. "Neurological Consequences of Neuroleptic Treatment of Autistic Children." (unpublished manuscript)

DiMascio, A.; Soltys, J.J.; and Shader, R.I. "Psychotropic Drug Side Effects in Children," in *Psychotropic Drug Side Effects*. R. Shader and A. DiMascio, eds. Williams and Wilkins, 1970, pp. 235-260.

9 Pharmacotherapy in geriatrics

Persons 65 and older constitute the fastest-growing segment of our population. In 1900, there were 3,000,000 of them in the United States population and in 1973, 20,000,000, 4 percent and 10 percent, respectively.

As a person enters this late stage of life, he changes the way he thinks, the way he feels about himself and his environment, and the way he reacts to that environment. Simple aging results from physiological, psychological, and social factors. And as aging progresses, the incidence of functional and organic behavioral disorders increases dramatically.

In a recent year, persons over 65 accounted for more than 300,000,000 physician visits—200,000,000 of them to primary physicians. Most often a geriatric patient first presents to a primary physician with a variety of physical and psychiatric signs and symptoms. The physician may wonder if he's confronted by physical disease with psychological concomitants or a psychological disorder with somatic concomitants. In either instance, a complete physical examination and appropriate laboratory assessments should be performed. Early recognition and treatment of simple aging problems are essential if the elderly patient is to continue functioning in his community. If he remains untreated or if pathological processes continue unchecked, he may develop severe psychiatric problems.

The incidence of psychiatric problems in the geriatric population is estimated to be as high as 85 percent. In various institutions there are more than 1,000,000 patients over age 65, and 80 percent or more display disabling psychiatric symptoms or signs of chronic brain syndrome. Twenty percent of all new mental hospital admissions are geriatric. Probably 40 percent of long-stay mental hospital patients are over 65, and the relative proportion is increasing as outpatient and community treatment programs for younger adults develop. One method of handling this problem is to reduce inpatient hospital populations by referring patients to nursing homes.

The common presenting complaints of patients who undergo simple aging are rarely seen alone. But they can be classified this way, for convenience sake:

Affective

> Anger
> Boredom
> Dependency
> Despair
> Disillusionment
> Loneliness
> Loss of self-esteem
> Somatic ailments

Behavioral

> Cantakerousness
> Compulsiveness
> Inability to cope with change
> Inappropriateness (actions not in keeping with the situation)
> Insomnia
> Self-destructiveness
> Stubbornness
> Uncooperativeness
> Withdrawal
> Agitation

Mental

> Confabulation (inventing stories to compensate for
>   memory losses)
> Confusion
> Disorientation
> Forgetfulness
> Intellectual deterioration

These complaints are rarely seen alone. The physician should determine the causes and treat accordingly whenever possible. Causative factors for the psychological problems of elderly patients fall into three categories:

Social

> Abandonment by family
> Decreased mobility
> Fear of losing economic security
> Lack of social interaction
> Inability to attain goals
> Loss of occupational interests and productivity
> Loss of role identity
> Reduced income

Psychological

> Reduced influence over environment
> Fear of "aloneness"
> Fear of death
> Loss of loved ones

Physiological

> Brain-tissue changes
> Decreasing motor strength
> Sensory losses (hearing, smell, taste, vision)

127

The primary goal of treatment should be to restore patients to a state of equilibrium. Environmental manipulation, supportive therapy, and psychotropic medication are usually combined to attain this goal. The common problems of simple aging can be mitigated by appropriate social, psychological, and physiological management. To that end, members of the health-care team should take actions like these:

Social

1. Encourage family involvement in the lives of elderly patients.
2. Arrange for financial counseling or assistance.
3. Encourage social interaction with others.
4. Stimulate their interest in hobbies.
5. Build geriatric patients' self-esteem by encouraging them to exercise, make decisions, take responsibility, and groom themselves.
6. Help them obtain part-time jobs.
7. Arrange for them to obtain improved housing.

Psychological

1. Manipulate their environment.
2. Provide psychotherapeutic counseling.
3. Prescribe psychotropic medications.

Physiological

1. Attempt to improve brain function with medications.
2. Correct sensory deficits whenever possible (refractions, cataract surgery, hearing tests).
3. Diagnose and treat underlying physical disorders.
4. Arrange for physical rehabilitation.

Psychiatric sequelae and complications

Mental deterioration in elderly patients often produces confusional states. Confusion is marked by forgetfulness, inadequate perception, disorientation, incoherence, wandering, agitation, and intractability. It is a complication of a disease process, not a diagnosis. For example, confusion may arise from cerebral hypoxia—but cerebral hypoxia may be precipitated by an intercurrent illness: fear, infection, dehydration, electrolyte imbalance, excessive alcohol consumption, drug intoxication, poor nutrition, or anemia.

If a patient continues to deteriorate, he may have to be admitted to a hospital or nursing home. However, this move to a clinical setting may add to his confused state because he is removed from familiar resources, deprived of tolerant family members and friends, and exposed to disapproval and alienation.

To help the patient counter his confusion and assist him in staying oriented, the physician and paramedical personnel should:

1. See to it that living arrangements have familiar or homelike touches: rooms individualized or readily identifiable by key colors, TVs and radios tuned to programs the patient likes, decorations displayed during holiday periods, and the like.
2. Insure that personal aids—glasses, dentures, and hearing aids—are available.
3. Provide patients with cues for orienting themselves: clocks, calendars on which dates can be marked off, newspapers, night-lights, and the like.
4. Maintain interpersonal relationships by listening and talking to patients, touching them, respecting them as

129

reasonable adults, giving them roommates, and providing social interactions.

Further deterioration may lead to marked behavior disturbances and emotional states, including a wish to die. More than 25 percent of all suicides are committed by elderly persons. Among other disorders are depression, delusions, and aggression (see Table 9-1, "Recognizing the causes of aberrant behavior"). It is at this stage that medication becomes a major treatment modality.

Treatment with medication

The aims of pharmacotherapy are:

1. To reduce psychiatric symptomatology and/or associated behavior, such as agitation, assaultiveness, anxiety, or changing moods, and to prevent suicide.
2. To reduce behavior manifestations of senile dementia: disturbed sleep, denudativeness, disorientation, and disruption of socialization and the self-care process.
3. To reverse the primary symptoms of senile dementia: intellectual deterioration, confusion, memory deficit, difficulties in communication, and perceptual-motor incoordination.

Physiological factors of aging call for precautions in the use of medications. In many ways geriatric patients respond to drugs like young children. Just as a child's enzyme systems, metabolic processes, and liver functions are less developed than those of an adult, so the elderly patient's are sluggish and deteriorating. Thus, in both cases, the body's ability to absorb, distribute, degrade, or eliminate drugs is impeded, and its susceptibility to side effects and toxic reactions enhanced.

130

For example, a common effect of aging is a decrease in absorptive ability. The gastrointestinal tract of an elderly person has fewer active cells and less blood flow than a younger person's. So fewer enzymes are needed for maintaining the transport mechanism, and the result is a slower absorption rate and slower build-up of the drug serum level. Therefore, a physician has to be cautious in building up dosages, so as not to overshoot the optimum level and arrive at a toxic level.

Another problem has to do with the distribution of drugs through the organism. Most psychotropic drugs are lipid-soluble. In older patients, fat tends to replace functional tissues, and this process causes the patient to be able to develop higher concentrations of drugs in the body and to retain them for longer periods of time.

Metabolic slowdown also affects dosage schedules. Demethylation, enzyme activity, serum albumin, and total binding sites drop off in older people, and they suffer from a high incidence of liver disorders. These conditions lead to impeded detoxification of drugs—and, therefore, to high plasma and tissue levels of unaltered and unbound medications. These conditions also result in the agents persisting in an elderly person's body for longer periods after discontinuation of the drug than they do in a younger person's.

Still another factor is decreased rate of elimination. Renal blood flow and glomerular filtration rate are slowed, too, with age, and even more so in patients on such agents as propranolol hydrochloride (Inderal, Inderide). Delay in elimination means a greater duration of drug activity.

With the pediatric analogy as a guideline, the prescribing physician can avoid serious pitfalls in coping with dosage sensitivity. Elderly patients often respond to quite small doses of medication—doses that would be considered inadequate in younger, newly hospitalized, acutely psychotic adults. Similarly, doses that would be considered of normal size for other adults may cause severe somnolence, ataxia, hypotension, or arrhythmia in elderly patients. The safest approach is to start off low and to gradually build the dosage to the point of clinical efficacy. Building up slowly is essential: Some patients with poor absorption may seem to tolerate rapid increases but, when serum level reflects the high doses achieved, these patients show adverse or toxic reactions.

On the other hand, it is equally important not to undertreat geriatric patients. The elderly person who has taken considerable quantities of a given medication—a chronic schizophrenic, for instance—may tolerate vastly greater doses than other individuals. The drug should be initiated at a low dose level and then adjusted upward within a few days if the target symptoms have not been alleviated; initially the total daily dose should be divided and administered a number of times throughout the day. Once the optimum dosage has been determined, and the target symptoms have responded, you can gradually shift the schedule to a once-daily bedtime dose. This tactic allows the patient to sleep better without hypnotics by taking advantage of the sedative properties of many psychotropic agents and tends to reduce the severity of undesirable side effects as well.

Medications effective for elderly patients fall into major categories: antipsychotics, antianxiety agents, antidepressants, cerebral circulation altering medications, and central nervous system stimulants.

Antipsychotics

Phenothiazines. Chlorpromazine (Thorazine) has

132

been most used in cases requiring control of agitation and hyperactivity, with or without other psychotic features. However, it may produce paradoxical effects like excitement and agitation—as well as hypotension, dizziness, oversedation, ECG changes, blood dyscrasias, and parkinsonlike tremors or rigidity.

Thioridazine hydrochloride (Mellaril), another phenothiazine, seems to be more universally accepted than chlorpromazine as an effective psychotropic for the elderly because it is less likely to produce adverse reactions. Mellaril can produce ECG changes very frequently, through their significance is unknown. A double-blind study done by Alvarez and his associates in more than 300 patients demonstrated that Mellaril reduced anxiety, agitation, depression, and tension and produced few side effects.

Acetophenazine maleate (Tindal) has not enjoyed much popularity with general clinicians. Yet studies reveal it to be quite effective and in geriatrics to cause few side effects, especially the extrapyramidal side effects (EPS) of other piperazine phenothiazines.

Trifluoperazine hydrochloride (Stelazine), perphenazine (Trilafon), and other piperazines have not found general acceptance. This is because their high potential for extrapyramidal side effects interferes with self-care and mobility.

Thioxanthenes. Chlorprothixene (Taractan) and thiothixene (Navane) have not been extensively adopted. But Taractan has been found valuable for patients who wake up early and remain awake, because it tends to prolong sleep. Navane may be useful in patients who are anergic and who do not need sedation. This drug can stimulate and activate patients. Unfortunately, staff

133

members of many institutions prefer an inactive, sedentary patient. Navane does not produce ECG changes—a definite plus for the drug—and is less likely than phenothiazines to cause other side effects, with the exception of extrapyramidal side effects, chiefly akathisia.

Butyrophenones. Haloperidol (Haldol) has proved effective in managing aggressiveness, agitation, and hyperactivity. Even though it does not produce ECG changes and seldom interacts with other drugs, it is responsible for a high incidence of extrapyramidal side effects and, therefore, is not so popular for geriatric cases.

Special precautions with antipsychotic drugs

The elderly are especially sensitive to cardiovascular side effects (hypotension and cardiac arrhythmias), blood dyscrasias, neurologic effects (parkinsonism and akathisia), and gastrointestinal problems (constipation and GI distress) resulting from antipsychotic medications. When these side effects occur, it is best to counter them by lowering medication dosages rather than adding drugs, like antiparkinson agents. The added anticholinergic effects of these drugs may cause bowel stasis, urinary retention, toxic deliria, or behavioral disturbances. When needed, they should be used sparingly and discontinued shortly after the extrapyramidal symptoms abate.

A serious problem of antipsychotic drugs—especially the phenothiazines—is their potential for producing a syndrome called tardive dyskinesia. The disorder is manifested in movements of the mouth, jaw, and tongue, often with grimacing, lip-smacking, and chewing. Such movements continue almost without letup except during sleep. Choreiform movements of the distal extremities and rocking movements of the trunk may also occur, but they are more common in younger patients than in the elderly.

Although phenomena of this sort have been observed for many years, they are more prevalent now and are clearly associated with use of antipsychotic drugs. The occurrence of the syndrome is greatest among older patients, especially women. An incidence of 2 to 5 percent in chronic geriatric wards or nursing homes is common. In one study, Greenblatt, Dominick, Stotsky, and Di-Mascio found an incidence of more than 60 percent in geriatric patients treated with phenothiazines in nursing homes.[1] And elderly patients have been known to develop this chronic disorder after only relatively brief exposure to antipsychotic drugs. Tardive dyskinesia is not improved by antiparkinson agents. While it may be temporarily suppressed by higher doses of antipsychotic drugs, it may often re-emerge. Thus neither of these approaches is recommended.

If a patient develops dyskinesia while on an antipsychotic agent, withdrawal may cause a temporary exacerbation of the dyskinesia. But conservative treatment consists of complete withdrawal from antipsychotic medication. The condition may then gradually ameliorate over months or years.

Antianxiety agents

Sedative-hypnotics. Considerable experience has shown that most barbiturates are contraindicated as antianxiety drugs and may cause oversedation and/or paradoxical excitement. However, a controlled study by Stotsky, Cole, and Tang demonstrated that butabarbital at 50 mg h.s. is an effective hypnotic, even producing some improvement in daytime ward behavior in chronic geriatric patients with sleep disorders.[2] Tolerance may be a problem if a barbiturate is continued for a long period.

Benzodiazepines. Chlordiazepoxide (Librium) and diazepam (Valium) have been used effectively in patients showing mainly anxiety and agitation. Paradoxical excitement, agitation, aggressiveness, confusion, and ataxia may occur, so the dosage should be set low initially and slowly increased. Another effective agent is oxazepam (Serax) which is rapidly biotransformed to an inactive product and does not accumulate in tissues to the same degree as the other drugs. Accordingly, it may be less of a problem during chronic therapy. Chlorazepate dipotassium (Tranxene), lorazepam (Ativan), and prazepam (Verstran) may also be effective, but because of their long-acting metabolites, therapeutic or toxic effects may be delayed in some patients.

Antidepressants

These agents are often employed to treat depression associated with senile dementia. However, differentiating depression from senile dementia and toxic states is crucial. Depression in the elderly may produce temporary confusion and memory deficits. But so may isolation, loneliness, physical deterioration, disturbed eating and sleeping, and a variety of drugs being prescribed for medical reasons—conditions that do not result from true depression and are not treatable with antidepressant drugs.

MAO inhibitors (Nardil and Parnate). The presence of increased levels of monoamine oxidase in the elderly suggests that MAO inhibitors may be useful. But they are actually being prescribed less and less often, because they tend to interact with other drugs, because they pro-

136

duce hypertensive crises when combined with foods high in tyramine, and because they occasionally produce acute hepatic insufficiency.

Tricyclics. Imipramine hydrochloride (Tofranil) and amitriptyline (Elavil) are valuable in treating geriatric depression. But because they cause ECG changes and hypotension, these drugs should be used cautiously in patients with cardiovascular disease. In addition, imipramine and its metabolite, desipramine hydrochloride (Norpramin, Pertofrane), may cause transient insomnia. As for amitriptyline, its sedating effects can produce drowsiness the next day and can impair mobility in the initial stages of treatment. Amitriptyline has the greatest anticholinergic activity of all the currently available tricyclic antidepressants, which can be a disadvantage.

Doxepin hydrochloride (Adapin, Sinequan) has been shown in studies by Goldberg and Finnerty to have considerable value, especially in patients with sleep disorders.[3] Doxepin has considerable antianxiety activity and does not produce ECG changes. Moreover, it has the fewest anticholinergic properties of all the antidepressants, making it more attractive for treatment of the elderly, whose physical conditions (glaucoma, lowered gastric mobility, and the like) preclude the use of drugs with anticholinergic actions.

Special precautions with antidepressants

1. Be sure to assess a patient's level of confusion prior to treatment. Toxic confusion is one side effect of these drugs.

2. Remember that atropinelike effects of tricyclic drugs are poorly tolerated. They increase susceptibility to

137

urinary retention and constipation, and may aggravate glaucoma.

3. Agitated depression occurs more frequently in old age than retarded depression; therefore, drugs with sedative actions often have greater utility.

4. Observe patients on antidepressants for decreased renal clearance and decreased threshold for Parkinson's disease.

5. Consider electroconvulsive therapy (ECT), which is still a highly effective treatment for depressed patients, especially those with serious cardiovascular disease. The cardiac stress produced by ECT under controlled conditions in the presence of a qualified anesthesiologist may be less severe than that produced by drugs such as Tofranil and Elavil. Though memory impairment from ECT may be exaggerated in elderly patients, it usually resolves fairly rapidly.

Cerebral circulation altering drugs (cerebral vasodilators)

Cerebral vasodilators are said to act by relaxing smooth muscles in blood-vessel walls, thereby increasing blood flow and oxygen supply to the brain. This assumes, however, a population of elderly individuals with inadequate brain blood supplies and dilatable nonsclerotic arteries. Yet vasodilators are often recommended for patients with arteriosclerosis, so their mechanism of action is open to question. In arteriosclerosis, damage to cerebral blood vessels reduces the ability of the vessels to dilate. Thus, blood actually flows to vessels that are *not* damaged and that are able to dilate. In addition, cerebral vasodilators are not suitable for severely disturbed patients.

138

The major drugs in this category are papaverine hydrochloride (Pavabid), cyclandelate (Cyclospasmol), and an ergot-alkaloid combination product (Hydergine). They are believed to increase cerebral blood flow without producing postural hypotension. It was hoped they would reverse intellectual deterioration and memory loss.

Papaverine hydrochloride (Pavabid). This drug is a non-narcotic alkaloid derivative of opium. Many studies attest to its usefulness, but few of them are double-blind. Pavabid generally benefits mildly impaired patients in early stages of illness, but it is relatively ineffective in treating intellectual impairment. It can also produce headaches, abdominal distress, flushing, and vertigo—but all of a mild nature. It is given in doses of 150 to 450 mg daily.

Cyclandelate (Cyclospasmol). Most widely used in Europe, it is said to improve communication, socialization, and orientation, but it has no effect on memory and perceptual motor skills. Ball and Taylor found that it improves long-term memory, reasoning, and orientation of mildly impaired patients in some mental function tests.[4] It seems to be well tolerated but can produce flushing, sweating, dizziness, drowsiness, and headache. It is used in doses of 800 to 1200 mg per day.

Ergot-alkaloid combination (Hydergine). Hydergine is a combination of three ergot derivatives and has also been administered extensively in Europe. The customary dosage is two to three 1.0-mg oral tablets daily.

Hydergine has been shown to be superior to placebo in six of seven studies, none of which extended longer than three months or employed a crossover control. In a study done at Cushing Hospital in Massachusetts, Banen found it improved ward behavior and general attitude but gave no improvement in intellectual functioning.[5] In another study measuring patients' daily activities, somatic complaints, mood states, and mental functioning, Gerin found that Hydergine diminished somatic complaints and improved patients' ability to perform the functions of daily life.[6]

The Medical Letter on Drugs and Therapeutics (March 1, 1974) concludes its evaluation of the agent as follows: "There is no convincing evidence that Hydergine has any value in the treatment of cerebral arteriosclerosis or senile behavior." However, about the same time, the National Academy of Science-National Research Council (NAS-NRC) review concluded that its evidence showed the drug to be effective for recommended indications. The new package insert states the drug is indicated for the treatment of selected symptoms in the elderly patient—mood depression, confusion, unsociability, dizziness—and that it can improve self-care.

Hydergine must be administered in frequent divided doses because it is short-acting. Nasal congestion and gastric distress are the main side effects, but these are generally minimal.

Anticoagulants as psychotropics

The principal anticoagulant is dicumarol. The rationale for its use is that it arrests the thrombotic process in arteries, veins, and capillaries—the cause of cerebral insufficiency—and thus increases blood flow. While it may alleviate symptoms initially, it also creates problems: Serious bleeding occurs in one-fourth of patients during treatment, and there is a high incidence of thromboembolic complications and fatalities when therapy is stopped.

140

Central nervous system stimulants as psychotropics

These drugs are tried in geriatric patients because such patients often are easily fatigued, have motor retardation, exhibit a decrease in drive and energy, and have reduced capacity for learning and concentration—all symptoms that are supposedly helped by stimulants. These drugs are also supposedly mood lifters, and geriatric patients are often lonely and depressed.

Pentylenetetrazol (Metrazol), and pipradol hydrochloride (Meratran), methylphenidate hydrochloride (Ritalin), deanol acetamidobenzoate (Deaner), and the amphetamines have all been applied because of their mild stimulant properties. They tend to produce a transient increase in patient activity and some improvement of intellectual functions. But these CNS stimulants are not true antidepressants. In general, studies of these drugs have produced equivocal results, and in actual practice they are seldom used. The clinician must beware that these medications do not increase confusion and paranoid ideations, especially at higher dosages. Nausea, vomiting, and headaches of a mild degree are the most common side effects.

Treatment suggestions for all psychotropics in geriatrics

1. Go slow in prescribing psychotropic drugs. Psychotropics may be contraindicated or may severely complicate treatment, because the elderly are subject to a high incidence of physical illness—cardiovascular disorders, respiratory problems, liver or renal dysfunctions, cancer, diabetes, or malnutrition. You should give careful physical examinations to patients before starting treatment,

141

and attack their medical conditions first. Do not overlook the possibility of delirium tremens; alcoholism is quite common in this age group.

2. Beware of drug interactions with nonpsychiatric medications. The most troublesome interactions are with these agents:

- Coumarin-type anticoagulants

- Thiazide diuretics, which may produce hypotensive crisis or renal insufficiency with Elavil or Thorazine

- Quinidine or steroids, which may cause an increase in psychopathological behavior

- Sleep medications, which increase confusion and delusional behavior

- Mineral oil, which may bind many lipid-soluble psychotropics, carry them out of the body, and thus diminish their actions.

3. Avoid polypharmacy with psychotropic drugs. Toxic psychological effects (delirium) and physiological effects (constipation, paralytic ileus, visual problems, urinary retention) can occur. A study of older patients by Leroyd showed that mental problems of those on five to 13 drugs improved when the number of agents was cut down.

4. Keep in mind that reserpine-induced depression is a common finding in hypertensive patients.

5. Select antipsychotic drugs generally to avoid specific side effects the drugs may cause rather than because of their therapeutic effects, since there is little difference in their over-all clinical effectiveness. In particular, try to avoid these serious side effects:

- Paralytic ileus which is provoked by anticholinergic actions

- Hypotension, which may precipitate myocardial infarction or predispose patients to cardiac arrhythmias—causing dizziness and loss of balance and, in turn, falls and fractures of fragile bones. (Do not, however, use epinephrine with phenothiazines to combat hypotension, as a paradoxical drop in blood pressure may result.)

6. Watch for extrapyramidal symptoms. Fifty percent of all patients older than 60 develop such symptoms, particularly akathisia and parkinsonism. These conditions are sometimes misdiagnosed as agitation or organic brain syndrome.

7. Note that chlorpromazine may lower the convulsive threshold in epileptic and brain-damaged patients.

8. Remember that the incidence of drug-induced agranulocytosis is related to old age (1:200 in the elderly as opposed to 1:6,000 in the general population). Threefourths of all patients with agranulocytosis are more than 50 years of age, and fatalities, too, increase with increasing age of patients. Fever, the best indicator, usually occurs within eight weeks.

Nonpharmacologic treatment of older patients

The pharmacologic approach to elderly patients is but one of several. We must provide for the patients, not the staffs of nursing homes or hospitals. Many staff members consider the ideal nursing-home patient to be self-feeding, continent, and otherwise inert, especially in homes that are often understaffed. If allowed, such personnel would prefer to "snow" patients, and that certainly is not in the patients' best interest.

By contrast, an active milieu with social activities, productive endeavors, occupational therapy, intellectual stimulation, family involvement, and individual counseling or therapy is more beneficial to patients. According to some investigators, providing beer or wine occasionally in a pub setting may increase socialization and reduce symptomatology.

Moreover, individual psychotherapy may help patients adjust to a new institutionalized setting or deal with feelings of impending death. Specific remedies include consulting with and educating nursing-home personnel to improve their understanding of patient dynamics and their handling of behavior problems.

144

Table 9-1

Recognizing the causes of aberrant behavior

How a patient acts	What it can mean
Cries periodically States he wishes to die States he feels hopeless Doesn't care for personal appearance Doesn't eat Can't sleep	Depression
Climbs into another patient's bed Removes clothes Extinguishes cigarettes on table Wanders aimlessly Urinates in room	Confusion

States someone is in the closet
    or under the bed
Refuses to eat or take medications,
    saying someone is trying to kill him
States a fixed but unrealistic belief
	Delusions

Threatens to hurt other patients Strikes out at staff Demands constant attention Shouts at staff and patients	Aggression
Refuses to leave his room Refuses to eat or sit with other patients Doesn't talk to anyone	Withdrawal

Paces in halls Constantly wrings hands Picks at bedclothes and self Constantly moves about when sitting	Agitation

Talks to "someone" who is not there Hears or sees an invisible person or object	Hallucinations

Can't give name Doesn't know the time or place Can't recognize familiar people	Disorientation

References

1. Greenblatt, D.L.; Dominick, J.R.; Stotsky, B.A.; and DiMascio, A. "Phenothiazine-Induced Dyskinesia in Nursing Home Patients." *J Am Geriatr Soc* 16:27, 1968.

2. Stotsky, B.; Cole, J.O.; Tang, Y.T. et al: "Sodium Butabarbital (Butisol Sodium) as a Hypnotic Agent for Aged Psychiatric Patients With Sleep Disorders." *J Am Geriatr Soc* 19:860, 1971.

3. Goldberg, H., and Finnerty, R. "Use of Doxepin in the Treatment of Symptoms of Anxiety Neuroses and Accompanying Depression: A Collaborative Controlled Study." *Am J Psychiat* 139:106, 1974.

4. Ball, J.A., and Taylor, A.R. "Effect of Cyclandelate of Mental Function and Cerebral Blood Flow in Elderly Patients." *Br Med J* 3:525, 1967.

5. Banen, D.M. "An Ergot Preparation (Hydergine) for Relief of Symptoms of Cerebrovascular Insufficiency." *J Am Geriatr Soc* 20:22, 1972.

6. Gerin, J. "Symptomatic Treatment of Cerebrovascular Insufficiency With Hydergine." *Curr Ther Res* 11:539, 1969.

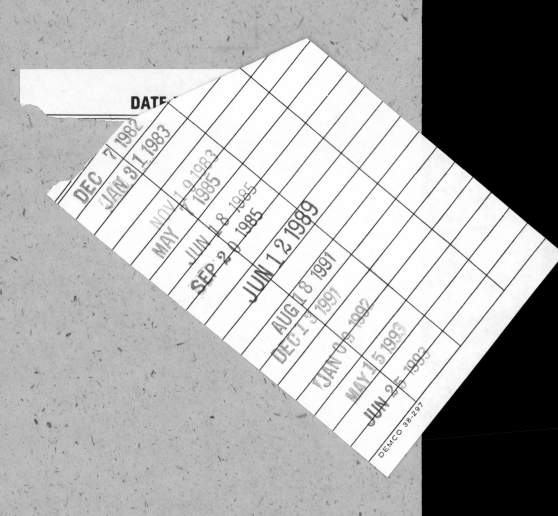